Saint Paul Almanac

Your Story Has Power: Tell It.

Saint Paul Almanac

Your Story Has Power: Tell It.

VOLUME 13

A PATH TO EACH OTHER

ARCATA PRESS

Saint Paul Almanac: A Path to Each Other, Volume 13
© 2022 Arcata Press

"Driving in West Saint Paul, Which Is South of Saint Paul but West of South Saint Paul" from *Honey in the Dark* by Lee Colin Thomas appears here by permission of Brighthorse Books, 2021.

"April in Minnesota" appeared in *Southwest Journal* (Mpls.) March 8–15, 2018.

"A Poem for Oliver" appeared in *The BeZine* online magazine.

"Dad's Grip" adapted from *His Father's Shirts* by George Slade appears here by permission of George Slade/PBW/GS Press.

ISBN: 978-0-9992077-4-1

Printed by Bookmobile

Saint Paul Almanac
275 East Fourth Street, Suite 701
Saint Paul, Minnesota 55101
saintpaulalmanac.org
Saint Paul Almanac is a subsidiarity of Arcata Press, a nonprofit publisher.

Saint Paul Almanac: A Path to Each Other

VOLUME 13 ❦ 2022

EXECUTIVE EDITORS
Wendy Brown-Baez (2021–2022)
Carolyn Holbrook (2019)

MANAGING EDITOR
Zoey Gulden

SENIOR EDITORS
Marion Gomez, Michael Kleber-Diggs,
Ben Weaver, Claudette M. Webster

YOUTH EDITOR
Kia Moua

COMMUNITY EDITORS
Mahemo Abakar, Ahmed Abdullahi, Leilani Andrews, Tomás Araya,
Colleen Casey, Alex Crawford, Bridget Geraghty, Casey Gordon,
Ibrahim Ibrahim, Alia Jeraj, Melody Luepke, Khalid Mohamed,
Marjorie Otto, Kathryn Pulley, Yusuf Sabtow, Ismail Sheikhomar,
Frankie Weaver, Aron Woldeslassie, Alexa Yankton, Lisa Yankton

COMMUNITY EDITOR PROJECT MANAGER
Shaquan Foster

EDITORIAL MATTERS
Anne Kelley Conklin: Copyeditor, proofreader
Steve Trimble: Quotations researcher

BOOK DESIGN AND PRODUCTION
Judy Gilats

PUBLISHER
Pamela R. Fletcher Bush

What Is Racism? Collage, Morgan Grayce Willow, 2020

Saint Paul Almanac: A Path to Each Other

VOLUME 13 ❦ 2022

is dedicated to

- Those who know that being in community is our strength and being authentically ourselves is our power
- Those who believe that peace starts with every choice we make
- Those who are envisioning and working toward change so our world becomes inclusive and equitable
- Those who are dedicated to making social justice a reality
- Those living with curiosity
- Those working tirelessly for the right of every person to feel safe, respected, and valued
- The compassionate who care for the vulnerable: the babies, the youth, and the older people; the unhoused and the incarcerated; and anyone who has been mistreated, displaced, or disregarded
- The stewards of Mother Earth who see that ecological justice is vital
- The independent thinkers and innovators who give us hope
- The storytellers speaking the truth so that we are provoked, inspired, and motivated to act

To each of you: we are grateful.

CONTENTS

Chapter 3: Fair & Foul Weather

Chapter 4: Family Matters

Chapter 5: Truth Telling

Chapter 6: Heart & Heartache

Chapter 7: Loving Our Neighbors

Chapter 8: Honoring Mother Earth

Passion and Purpose Create a Book

Saint Paul Almanac Community Editor Apprenticeship Project

WENDY BROWN-BAEZ

IF YOU WANT TO UNDERSTAND the mission of *Saint Paul Almanac*, consider the following:

- More than eighty languages are spoken in Saint Paul public schools.*
- Saint Paul's population is 64.3% White non-Hispanic, 13.4% Asian, 12.6% African American and Pan African, 8.5% Hispanic, and 1.2% American Indian.*
- Rondo Days is an African American celebration that commemorates the history and legacy of Rondo. By the mid-1800s, Rondo had become the heart of the Saint Paul African American community. This community flourished until 1956, when the federal government built Interstate 94 through Rondo, destroying Black businesses and residences. Today, with established homes and businesses and active community leaders, the heart of Rondo is alive and thriving.
- The city of Saint Paul is on the original homeland of the Dakota people, where they live and work today along with their relatives from the Ojibwe, Ho-Chunk, Iowa, and many other tribes. Later Saint Paul became occupied predominantly by French, German, and Irish Catholic communities while Minneapolis became occupied by Scandinavians and Lutherans. Today, the Twin Cities are

---

*"About Saint Paul," Saint Paul, Minnesota, accessed Nov. 14, 2020, stpaul.gov.

home to recent immigrant communities, including Cameroonian, Hmong, Liberian, Oromo, and Somali groups.

What do facts have to do with storytelling? When you look at these facts, you see that the voices of all the people who make up the neighborhoods of Saint Paul are vital to the past and current historical record and legacy of the city.

The community editor apprenticeship provides a way for people from diverse backgrounds to come together and have conversations about cultural sensitivity, equity, and social justice, and our role in creating change as individuals and as a literary journal. Apprentices come from a variety of ethnic and socioeconomic backgrounds, ages, genders, gender identities, and levels of writing experience. It's imperative to acknowledge the history of BIPOC, LGBTQIA, and differently abled communities throughout our conversations about individual pieces. Doing so, we collect and publish stories representative of the people and places of Saint Paul, choosing those that are the most engaging, provocative, or heartfelt from the more than 400 submissions we receive each year.

The process itself is more complicated than you might think. Twenty editors meet in small groups to learn what editing entails, to create and use a basic rubric, and to discuss the merits and flaws of each submission. We also learn how to solicit stories, and we have an opportunity to champion one piece to the entire group at the end.

Given this explanation, the editorial process may appear mundane. But, in fact, our discussions are lively, even boisterous, thought provoking, stimulating, and emotional as we get to know each other weekly over a period of three months. We have a rare opportunity to see the world with new perspectives, through someone else's eyes. We often read stories from the point of view of someone who is experiencing or resisting oppression. In learning about each other's cultures and histories, sometimes we must reevaluate our own stereotypical thinking and biases. We may not always agree, but we agree to listen. We gain a new understanding of how current events impact the youth, and we enter doorways into personal and collective grief. When we read about family traditions, we smile or sigh or feel intrigued. We explore what makes a poem really sing. We read odes to the city and to natural settings of parks, lakes, and the river. We learn that important stories can be edited and revised to become well-crafted, influential works. The heart of our work is to dialogue with each other. What is a Saint Paul story or a Saint Paul voice? What stories are missing? How do we find those stories?

Stories empower us when we tell them, and they empower the potential for change when others hear them. We are hardwired for stories. Scientists have discovered that when we read stories, our brains produce the hormones that deepen bonding and foster compassion. This is the beginning of transformation and the possibility of justice, when we read something that makes us stop and think, or acknowledges the work we are doing or could be doing toward building community.

We love to hear a good story and let it sink in so deeply it is never forgotten; to be moved by a poem that heartens and lifts us up. We are reminded of life's good when we read someone's appreciation for simple things, such as a family recipe or kindness toward a neighbor. We are inspired by stories of resiliency during tough times, and we are stirred by encounters with the natural world. We feel outraged at injustice, and we celebrate what is endearing and enduring.

The community editor project is the first step in getting these stories out into the world, where they can be savored and where, hopefully, you too will be motivated to ask yourself: What makes a neighborhood thrive? What turns a place into a home? How can we flourish individually and collectively? What stories have we not yet heard, and how can we deepen our attention?

For me, personally, being a part of this circle has been eye-opening, invigorating, and fulfilling. What I learn is invaluable. I become more well informed and a better citizen as a member of society and as a member of our literary community. More than anything else, the community editor project gives me hope. Besides the pleasure of getting to know remarkable individuals, I see what is possible when we join with passion and purpose.

Saint Paul Almanac is a literary-centered arts organization. We share stories across cultures and cultivate dialogue to promote understanding, relationships, and collaborative action. Our mission is primarily accomplished through collaborative decision-making in publication activities, readings, and mentorships that develop, amplify, and honor local voices.

To learn more about the community editor project, please go to https://saintpaulalmanac.org/projects/community-editor -apprenticeship/.

Publisher's Note

PAMELA R. FLETCHER BUSH

2020. JUST THE MERE MENTION of this historic year still blows the minds of everyone I know. On January 7, I anticipated and envisioned the exciting work in store for me as I eagerly assumed leadership at Saint Paul Almanac (SPA). Yet, in March, the COVID-19 pandemic produced a new reality for the entire world. It changed how we lived and worked. We could no longer rely on our established routines, expectations, and aspirations as 2020 became a time unlike any other in our contemporary society. In a concentrated period, we encountered heightened fear, antagonism, and personal violence; isolation and loneliness due to social distancing and quarantining; illness, dying, and death; hunger, eviction, and homelessness; lost wages and unemployment; gendered and racialized strife and violence; police brutality, the murder of Mr. George Floyd, and the resultant worldwide protest against racial injustice; and the contentious 2020 election of President Joe Biden that divided the country, and the ensuing fallout constricting voting rights. The list rolls on.

I soon learned, however, that tough times toughen the resolve of compassionate, concerned people. The synergy of creative and resourceful leaders from various community arts organizations, other nonprofits, the business sector, charitable organizations, and individual donors created a significant force to support the arts on both moral and financial levels. Their efforts benefited SPA immensely, helping us stay open and save our stories. In March, we moved our publishing program online to our social media platforms; we published thirty-second stories about surviving social distancing and quarantining, stories of Black writers in response to the murder of Mr. George Floyd, and the writing and visual artwork of our Freedom Forward (July 4) contest winners. We also reprinted archived work of previous *Almanac* volumes.

Despite operating with reduced funding in a time of economic urgency and social/political upheaval, we thrived by squeezing so much from the limited resources we had acquired and dared to look toward 2021 with hope. At the end of 2020, we celebrated with a virtual block party featuring a multifaceted group of poets, writers, musicians, and filmmakers.

2021. At the beginning of the year, while Omicron, the new COVID-19 variant was spreading so easily, everyone I knew hoped for a return to normalcy. However, on January 6, an attempted coup on the United States Capitol to overturn the 2020 presidential election occurred. Despite it all, I began the new year by planning an annual community fundraising strategy to gain the funds needed to publish *Almanac*, Volume 13, and future volumes. With the help of the SPA development and marketing committees, we worked to implement this strategy.

Meanwhile, in June, undeterred by our country's divisive atmosphere, the U.S. Senate and the House of Representatives voted to make Juneteenth the eleventh annual national holiday on the federal calendar.

In September, we launched Almanac Accolades, our sustaining monthly membership drive, acquiring sixteen members to support our ongoing book production! In October, we launched the Carol Connolly Initiative for Almanac Poets and Writers to support our contributors. We wrapped up our annual campaign in November by launching the Nightingale Tilsen Legacy Fund to raise funds to print and distribute the *Almanac*.

During these three inaugural fall fundraising campaigns, you, our beloved Saint Paul Almanac community, contributed generously and sacrificially. Thank you for your support during such economically challenging times! You're indispensable to us, so we don't take your invaluable participation and support for granted, whether you contribute through your dollars, submissions, purchases, or volunteer time. Please continue to consider how SPA benefits you, your family, and our community, and continue to give what you can.

During this blessed and complicated year, we also received an extraordinary invitation to partner with the Minnesota Humanities Center (MHC), a committed funder that has supported us throughout the years. This unique partnership came with a tremendous gift earmarked to help publish and promote *Almanac* Volume 13! Such an opportunity to collaborate with MHC in this way arrived at a most auspicious time for SPA.

2022. Today Saint Paul Almanac is thrilled to launch *Almanac*, Volume 13: *A Path to Each Other*. The title of this volume stems from Julia Klatt Singer's pithy and potent two-line poem "Stones," which is published in this book. When I read the poem, the few words filled my mind with a question that Klatt Singer seems to pose: Violence or peace? Did the pandemic just unleash the virulent conflict already lurking beneath the surface, or did American society suddenly change? History reveals that societal struggles are constant and embedded in our culture. There's no question that our society is visibly polarized across cultural, gendered, national, political, racial, and socioeconomic lines, among others. A vivid example of polarization and its tragic and far-reaching impact on the world is the current Russian invasion of Ukraine. There and in other war-torn countries, we witness how imperialism begets both physical and psychic harm.

What can Saint Paul Almanac do to help counteract polarization? Its founder, Kimberly Nightingale, stated in her final publisher's note in Volume 12: "My goal was that the Almanac be a part of an equity-grounded, full quality-of-life value system. Minnesota is still a land of segregation in so many of our organizations and businesses. We are often defensive and resistant to change." Following this statement,

Nightingale posits that change and justice are possible when we are intentional in our efforts to work together for the common good.

Twelve years ago, in the fall of 2010, I was invited to join SPA's Board of Directors. I accepted the invitation because, as a writer, I was intrigued and inspired by the organization's mission to effect change through storytelling. I was especially drawn to the community editor project, an inclusive process I'd never seen before. As an editor, I wanted to be involved in that action, so I applied to be a community editor. Working in tandem with the other editors and writers became a highlight of my creative life. Over time, I enjoyed the privilege of working as a co-senior editor and later as the executive editor of *Saint Paul Almanac*. Now, in this new generation of Saint Paul Almanac, I'm honored to be at its helm, continuing to lay a path that leads to a place where individuals across the spectrum of our society can come together to use words to build and uplift each other and our communities.

May you enjoy reading this new volume of *Almanac*! Please promote and share it to keep our stories alive.

Saint Paul Almanac Board of Directors

Justin Holt, Board Chair
Stewart Stone, Secretary/Nominations Chair
Carla Knight, Treasurer
Marion Gomez, Development Chair
Katie Vagnino, Marketing Chair
Claudette Webster, Education and Program Chair
Damien Mills, Education and Program Committee

Special shout-outs to the committee members who volunteered their time to help produce the successful 2021 fall campaigns: Marion Gomez, development chair; Wendy Brown-Baez, a member of the development committee; Katie Vagnino, marketing chair; and Jordan Hirsch, a member of the marketing committee. Many thanks to the entire board for their vote of confidence that is encouraging me to take Saint Paul Almanac to the next level.

Book Note
and Land Acknowledgment

WINNING POEMS OF THE 2021 Sidewalk Poems Contest appear throughout the book as a collaboration between Saint Paul Almanac and Public Art Saint Paul. Public Art Saint Paul works with artists and community members to bring art into everyday life and to bring people together, fostering a more engaged social sphere.

This art project was originated by Public Art Saint Paul City Artist Marcus Young in 2008 and started under the name "Everyday Poems for City Sidewalks." Sidewalk poetry continues as an ongoing, systems-based work of art and the vanguard expression of the pioneering idea of "City Art." This project reimagines Saint Paul's annual sidewalk maintenance program as an ongoing publishing entity for a city-sized book of poetry. Sidewalk poetry allows city residents to claim the sidewalks as their book pages by creating moments of contemplation and reflection through these poems.

Arcata Press|Saint Paul Almanac pay homage to Mni Sóta Maḳoce–Dakota Homeland, on which these sidewalk poems are stamped and where we live, recreate, and work. Despite the brutal colonization they have endured over the centuries, the Dakota people remain alive and resilient and continue to thrive. To those of you who are reading this book, we invite you to join SPA in standing and working with the Dakota people to help create a society of equity and freedom for everyone. At this moment, think about donating at least $5 to a Saint Paul Native–governed organization. Here is a short list to consider: Ain Dah Yung Center, American Indian Family Center, American Indian Cancer Foundation, and Women of Nations' Eagles Nest Shelter. Thank you for your consideration and action.

Cover Note

George Morrison
Untitled (Lake Superior Landscape)
1986, acrylic on canvas | 47¾ x 47⅛ inches
Minnesota Museum of American Art Collection
Katherine G. Ordway Fund Purchase
© Briand Morrison

GEORGE MORRISON, the acclaimed Ojibwe artist, grew up in Chippewa City, Minnesota, and became a founding figure of Native American modernism. His illustrious and vast array of works include paintings, drawings, rubbings, lithographs, sculptures, and monumental wood collages made from found objects. Morrison is best known for his collages, such as *Cumulated Landscape*, and his abstract landscapes, such as *Untitled (Lake Superior)*. He held his first solo shows in Manhattan in 1948, resulting in twelve one-person shows in New York between 1948 and 1960. In the 1980s and 1990s, he worked prolifically and earned several noteworthy public commissions. He also exhibited his large sculpture *Red Totem* at the White House in 1980. Furthermore, Morrison received the first Master Artist Award in the Eiteljorg Museum's Fellowship for Native American Fine Arts in 1999.

On April 22, 2022, the U.S. Postal Service unveiled the George Morrison Forever stamps at a First Day Release Ceremony. Five of Morrison's artworks are displayed in a pane of twenty stamps.

REFERENCES
Newsroom, The United States Postal Service. 2021. "National News Release: George Morrison."
Rushing, W. Jackson, Rushing, W. Jackson III, and Kristin Makholm. 2013. *Modern Spirit: The Art of George Morrison*. Norman, Oklahoma: University of Oklahoma Press.

CHAPTER 1
CITY SHAPES

"Having moved from Pittsburgh to Saint Paul, I felt I could hear voices for the first time accurately."
—*August Wilson, award winning playwright, writer of* Fences

"I think it is generally admitted that Saint Paul among midwestern cities was not quite like the other girls, but that she has a definite personality and flavor of her own."
—*Grace Flandrau, novelist and writer*

"Of all the American regions, the Midwest remains the most imaginary, ahistorical but fiercely emblematic. It's Nowheresville. But it's also the Heartland."
—*Patricia Hampl, writer, essayist, and memoirist*

The City I Grew Up In

ARIA DOMINGUEZ

The city I grew up in is gone.
I recognize avenue names,
landmarks that remain undemolished,
but the landscape is no longer familiar to my soul.
It is not what the child I was called home.
Vacant lots with tossed tires and rotting couches
have been erased by shining condos.
Weed trees have been ripped up, replaced
with landscaped perfection. Peeling,
cracking siding has been hidden
behind smooth vinyl, graffiti obliterated
with coats of fresh paint, streets freshly paved,
sidewalks recently poured, sod freshly laid.
Bizarre mirages have appeared, oases in what was an
economic desert: natural foods co-op, bookstore,
brewery, music school, even a vegan restaurant
across from a coffee shop at Selby and Victoria.
These are not the gritty streets that held me
as I struggled to make my way through the world,
the ones where I was mugged and propositioned
walking back from the school bus,
where summer nights crackled with gunshots and illegal fireworks,
where certain intersections were strictly forbidden.
Where have the girls like me gone?
There must be a place where forgotten kids roam
decaying neighborhoods in hand-me-down clothes
on a banana seat bike, hitting potholes for fun,
trying to avoid the men who wash up in places like that.
But the city I grew up in is gone.

Driving in West Saint Paul, Which Is South of Saint Paul but West of South Saint Paul

LEE COLIN THOMAS

What part of the city is this?
I asked, suspicious that the GPS
was playing cat's cradle with us.

It's a mystery, you said, looking past
the windshield to a handful of pennies
tossed on the road, a disruption of light

along that bluff above where the river
flexes against its banks, and voluminous
greens arch backs to indigo hands

reaching out from the dusk. Not so
very long ago, you and I were both
infants. Crazy, isn't it? Those bodies

became these bodies. The wet little yolks
of our souls lived unsettled inside
a nest of new ribs, and we slept

unaware the runny things
would have to sustain us
for a lifetime. Maybe longer.

What did we think? Waking
inside this simmer of bright
to a world—unnamed, wild,

endless with bruise and flowers,
blizzard, chrome, darkness
thick as syrup. Heat dance

behind the curtain, sour light
and so much beyond reach.
Of course we cried. And then

we continued on. Seeing
what we would see. Going
where we could go.

Old Man Down

DAVID RALPH JOHNSON

THE STATE CAPITOL DOME reflected briefly in the history museum's north windows as I darted by. Its white marble curves followed the arch of the museum windows in perfect harmony. I would recall this later, but just then had no time to ponder anything but my hair-raising descent on two wheels down Twelfth Street and over the freeway. Destination Lowertown.

I had taken training earlier in the day on the capitol mall to learn how to safely ride an e-scooter. Two young Department of Public Safety staffers, fit and tech savvy, provided instruction to me and a small group of my Department of Transportation coworkers. They began by telling how to start an e-scooter with a mobile phone. Sound advice followed. "Wear a suitable helmet. Test the brakes *before* you get rolling. Top speed of fifteen miles an hour is *not* the time to realize you're missing either one." After some questions and answers, they each got on one, hit the throttles, and circled us in convincing smooth steady lines.

Now it was our turn. A few daring souls gave the e-scooters a try. I watched as they did very well, looping the mall plaza like a kettle of land hawks gliding the capitol terrain with ease.

On foot to my apartment after work, I came upon a freestanding e-scooter. By chance, a kid whizzed by riding one of the same. He was crouched to break the wind, milking as much speed out of the skinny rig as possible. Inspired, my eighteen-year-old brain kicked in and jumped my sixty-six-year-old body onto the e-scooter platform next to me. Startup engaged, I was gone.

What an amazing ride. After mastering the Twelfth Street descent, I flew the city streets unfettered on electronic power sent from web-enabled heaven. The Jackson Street bikeway was reached in two minutes. South on its two open lanes took me straight to Fifth Street, then a hard left pointed me home.

The expression on my face and those of passing bystanders melded into white toothy blurs.

My pedestrian days were over. This had to be shared. I stopped a block from the apartment and rang my wife.

"Hello."

"Jill, look out the window."

"Why, Anthony?"

"You'll see."

I hung up, remounted my chariot of fire, and took off.

Jill caught my approach from our window two stories up from Mears Park and gave me one of her what-the-heck-now-Anthony waves.

Wave returned, I slowed to a crawl and readied to park. In the process, my front tire buried itself in the wood chips of a sidewalk tree and sent me crashing to the cement.

Kids on a park bench yelled, "Hey, old man down."

I rolled and popped upright. Hearing their alert, I scanned the area to help the older man. Realizing the person of their concern was me, I gave them a not-to-worry thumbs-up.

One kid tossed a "nice recovery" back at me. I felt somewhat less old with that.

Given no broken body parts, Jill wasn't too upset when I got upstairs, saying, "Nice joke, Anthony, but you could've killed yourself."

Old man down, not old man dead. So far, so good in Lowertown.

August Breeze

MARJORIE OTTO

On a cool August evening, I walk down Greenbrier Street
where the breeze blows through open windows.
It's that time of year
where A/Cs are shut off and windows reopen
to soak up the last bit of summer.
Opened windows extend living rooms, kitchens
to the street where we all share
the smells of dinnertime, the laughs, the arguments.
Snippets of each other's lives ride on the breeze.

The Mountain and the New Part

PAUL BARD

FOR ONE GLORIOUS WINTER we went sliding anytime we wanted, without having to ask our parents for a ride to Highland. Yes, it was pretty cool growing up across the street from a mountain—even if it was only there for one year.

In my first-grade class at Nativity Grade School, most of the kids only saw the mountain from a distance, during recess. But I got to see it up close every day and watch as it grew from a little pile of dirt. That was just one of the benefits of living on Wellesley, between Fairview and Prior in 1960. The old part of Nativity looked pretty ancient back then, with its red brick and Gothic arches. After all, it had been built in 1923. The New Part, on the other hand, was to be a gleaming, modern addition, with sleek aluminum windows and a huge new gym. But before the New Part could go up, six houses had to be cleared out of the way, including ours.

We lived at 1877 Wellesley, on the same side of the street as Nativity. Two houses next to us and three behind us on Stanford all had to go. Most of them were moved. I remember seeing a house on wheels creeping out into the street, turning slowly, and going down the block, off to parts unknown. Others followed. But our house, the oldest and smallest, was apparently, in the opinion of grown-ups who decide such things, not worth moving. So, ours alone among the six was torn down. I saw the wrecking ball crash into the chimney one day as I was walking home from school. Sad, yes. But in the eyes of a six-year-old, watching that collision was actually pretty cool. That coolness outweighed the sadness of seeing the old house go. Besides, our new house—we'd moved directly across the street— was bigger and nicer than the old one. And once the houses were gone, up rose the mountain.

When excavation for the New Part's foundation began, all that dirt had to go somewhere. The pile rose higher and higher every day, until it was taller than the houses around it. Days and days were spent climbing and exploring through that summer and fall. Then came winter and with it, winter's snow. Kids from up and down the block brought sleds, toboggans, flying saucers, and pieces of cardboard to go up and down, up and down, hour after hour. Some older kids even brought skis. Skis! We were the luckiest, though, because the mountain was right across the street.

We hoped winter would never end. But winter led to spring and our mountain turned to mud. Months passed, and as the New Part grew, the mountain slowly shrank away. A brand-new blacktop playground took its place. Organized softball games, though, could never match the adventure of the mountain and the drama of its rise and fall.

City Sonnet

MARY TURCK

A sonnet's fourteen lines loop back between behind
some hard-won truth burning blazing brighter than
daily duties diaries discussions disappointments
beacon in the dark night of the soul of the
sole writer thinker reader true believer in birds and trees
and rivers as the Crow flows twists turns forks as
the Mississippi meanders until the West Side lies
east of the rest of the city just to confuse bemuse befuddle
true believers in geography as destiny and direction as definition
before the birth of Google death of maps
certainty without sight or study
West is East and Frogtown is French and Saint Paul was
laid out long ago, late at night, beery bigwigs tangling
towns and streets and looping back between behind again.

Salad, A Vignette

SARAH KOPER

As I LOOK OUT of my fifth-story window at the Saint Paul landscape below, I think of salad, tossed salad. More specifically tossed salad of green, red, and oak leaf lettuce, kale, spinach, romaine, an occasional clump of radicchio, and unruly fronds of arugula. Arugula reminds me of opera. Sing, "arugula, arugula, arugula." Pavarotti would do it justice. Clearly, I cannot. Here and there rooftops protruding above the tree line remind me of croutons, garlic preferred. Yum. Hungry, I salivate. Fortunately for Saint Paul, I am not hungry enough to eat a whole city today.

Frantic

ARON WOLDESLASSIE

I'M IN GREAT SHAPE, but the only exercise I get is from running late. Today's disaster is a job interview in some Lowertown bakery. The job came from a friend who saw the previous baker add a touch too much salt to the sourdough after inadvertently slicing his hand open. The job opened like the window of an eclipse.

I'm an eager beaver, so I book it down Snelling. From there it's the A Line to the Green Line, then a short walk to the bakery. Everything's coming together when for some reason the A Line passes me. It passes me. It. Passes. Me. The interview is in forty minutes and I'm some six miles from the bakery.

Now, a car person would hear that and go, "Six miles? You've got plenty of time! Grab a drink, relax, and drive there in 30 minutes, ya goof." But us bus people hear that and go, "Six miles? You should have been on the bus twenty minutes ago, ya goof."

Frantic, I run down Snelling. I'm in triage mode. Maybe I can get on the 74 and ride it all the way into the city. But I gotta run fast because the 74 is a slippery bus. Sometimes it's four minutes early, other times it's six minutes late.

Chugging along the street, new questions and corresponding answers come to mind. They'll ask, "Why were you late?" and when I explain that my father died, fake tears will help sell the lie. They'll say, "You're sweating; did you run here?" To that, I'll laugh and explain how I perform lunges to help keep myself ready for anything. They'll wonder, "Do you often exercise after the death of a loved one?" The answer to that doesn't come to me because I'm too angry at the 74 bus that appears seven minutes early!

Are you kidding me, God? You give Celine Dion five Grammys and I can't get a single ride? With the bus gone, I have to spend money to make money: I order a ride. The little app says it'll be seven minutes before my driver arrives. As I wait, another A Line bus drives by. This one stops at its stop.

The little car on my phone isn't moving. It's been circling the block for some reason. I'm panicking. Time is not my friend here. Nine minutes later, Marcus appears, unaware that he's late.

"Hey, how we doin'?" he asks, oblivious to the man-made stop signs.

"Oh, I'm good, thanks."

"Where you headed?"

The app says where I'm going. He nods and the car moves forward. Short on time doesn't make for a good commute. There's a part of me that wants to scream at every red light. My ten-minute ride takes me roughly eleven minutes.

That's great. It's fine. I'm okay.

Through the door of the bakery a rush of warm air and hearty scents hit me. A flaxen-haired woman watches me look around.

"Hello," she says in a breathy timbre, "what can I get you today?"

A rehearsed smile spreads across my face as I approach. The right thing to say would be, "Hello my name is so-and-so I'm here for a job interview. Look at how early I am, I'm exceptional." Among the delicious scents of bread and croissants is something foul and familiar: me. My nerves and running have resulted in a bit of sweat.

So I ask, "Do you have a bathroom I can use?" She points and I power walk to the tiny tiled room. Quickly I take off my shirt and take what was once called a whore's bath which progressives later renamed a bum's bath and then renamed to sink bath. Soap and water in hand, I dab my pits clean until the smell fades.

I take a breath, wink at the handsome fella in the mirror, and turn the knob to the exit only for the knob to keep turning. Strange. I keep turning the knob only for it to keep spinning in place.

I twist, it turns. I twist again; it turns again. I twist with passion, gusto, and verve and it turns off of the door. The handsome man in the mirror looks at me, flabbergasted. Pushing on the door, I learn it's still locked.

God, possibly angry about the Celine Dion thing, has given me a locked door. But when the devious creator closes a door, he opens a window. Turning around, I look for a window. There aren't any windows, but there are stalls. Lots of stalls. Too many stalls for any men's room.

"Hello?" I ask the hopefully empty women's room.

"Hello?" replies a confused voice from one of the stalls.

It doesn't matter how early I arrive or how good I smell, if I trap myself in the women's room, I won't get the job. I kick the door like a cop in a movie. The wood splinters but doesn't break. I kick again, I kick a third time, and the door flings open, hallelujah!

Sprinting to the counter, I introduce myself to the blonde before asking for the owner.

"The owner? She'll be a sec; she just went to the bathroom."

I gasp.

"What's wrong?"

Behind me is the voice from the stall repeating with grumbling disdain, "Hello."

Ax-Man Surplus Sandbox

MAE WHITNEY

AH, AX-MAN SURPLUS STORES: home of doodads, baby legs, Velcro, out-of-date calendars, misprinted wedding mementos, and wholesale hardware. Anyone with a lick of creative juice in their blood can find something to fulfill a long-ago pinned Pinterest wish. With the incredible varying array of products, they've attracted a diverse crowd for over fifty years. Their website states that they have "a loyal following of local artists, tinkerers, engineers, makers, and freaks and geeks of all styles." My dad used to take me as a kid—I'd ask where all this random stuff came from. "Fell off the back of a truck somewhere," he told me. This isn't far from the truth. Their supplies come from any number of manufacturers whose last chance to make their money back on a bum batch is selling these goods at cost to Ax-Man.

Puns, fart jokes, and political jabs written in Sharpie on cardboard and neon labels dot the aisles. They identify merchandise and read "I'm sure they're good for something" above barrels of marbles and "Nun Weapons" beside a basket of crucifixes. Ax-Man: home to the work of humorists that make you wonder, was a portfolio of bathroom graffiti required upon application for employment? The humor inspiring the various doodles that accompany these labels are left over from a bygone era when crust-punk/hippy/straightedges knew no bounds and victoriously proclaimed, "I AM CAMP; HEAR ME ROAR!"

Spotting the adult humor and obscene depictions of George W. Bush as a kid was akin to skipping to the back of *City Pages* to read the "Savage Love" advice column, next to the racy ads. I'd snag a copy on our way out with my pockets full of tiny potion bottles and new stickers to adorn my Beach Cruiser. I'd bring my new trinkets and rolled-up *City Pages* to my friends while we tinkered and read all about the scandalous love lives of adults. At this point, I'd like to insist that Ax-Man is, in fact, kid friendly. The aisles are already a mess with somewhat broken merchandise, so an accompanied adult need not worry about the "you break it, you bought it" rule. Send those curious minds in with a roll of quarters, and they will come out with a basket of odds and ends that they intend on turning into the best invention or work of art they can think of. While you're there, let your mind wander and hands touch, and select an item that sparks childlike engagement—Ax-Man: a sandbox for the minds of people at any age.

Friday the Recycling Truck

JOHN MINCZESKI

grinds to our house,
gorging on castoffs—newspapers,
magazines that have lost
their flavor—bestowing
its weekly absolution.
For penance, I roll the bin back
to the side of the garage.
It is democratic, this ritual
an hour after the garbage truck,
that creature of landfills.
It groans along, breaking
the threads of Friday quiet,
our scavenger beetle
dragging its thorax
through this loop
of Parkview Lane.
Here's proof, through all
the clamor and growl,
we thrive through entropy.
The driver, high priest,
raises the hydraulic arm in blessing.
The stock market is up slightly,
the economy steams along.
Behind these diesel fumes,
our hope is ever elastic.

Saint Paul Uses She/Her Pronouns

ANNETTE MARIE SMITH

The city has the fae about her,
sways her hips in the way
the wind moves the trees
and the trains
undulate along their sinuous tracks.
She sings softly to herself as rain plinks
into fountains and shivers into cracks,
the low cadence of her voice,
a hum really,
mute of words but full of bat squeaks
and bird trills
of sirens wailing like banshees
and the dull roar of locomotives,
prayers really,
in her pagan dialect.
Her name is something holy and masculine
but the halo she wears is really a crown
spiked with rays of lights emanating from many jewels profane,
Allianz Field, Xcel Energy Center, The Palace Theatre,
to name a few.
She is ultimately fluid, a shapeshifter/selkie,
but with her feet always rooted in the Mississippi River.
Saint Paul puts her fingers to her
red light red lips
and blows kisses to the moon.

Coffee Ode

HANNAH BOEHME

This place called to me. It made me feel at home in my bones.
It was the aching blue sky, forced between brick-walled buildings
    but fighting to reach me anyway.
I felt it in the soft hum of bees and the scrape of plastic chairs on
    cobblestone, in the plants that sprouted in this urban space, with
    both help and hindrance from the people sharing this place.
    The steam of coffees warm in hand would coil upwards, away,
    longing to join the sky above.
The rain always seemed to catch me in this place, soft and gray and
    inviting. It would patter against the umbrella's canopy and I
    would sit for a few minutes, not yet driven inside.
Watch the clear drops trace along every leaf of the wall ivy,
And remember to breathe
In the midst of my tangled life
It was a time to just be.

This space is no longer there
—not exactly as it was—
The sky has expanded, reclaimed this place
That wall of ivy has toppled and now it is something new
The coffee's steam still rises into the misty air
Though it is forever changed.
Yet something of this place remains
In me
Reminding me to breathe

Rondo Avenue: The Rhythm of Life

MARGARET PONDER LOVEJOY, EdD

THERE ARE MANY STORIES and accounts of the old Rondo Avenue. Most notable, it was more than just a street. It was an entire community. From Rice to Lexington, Selby to University, Rondo was alive with various establishments. But most of all, it was the spirit of the people.

All the streets were tree-lined, especially Rondo Avenue, which was arched with graceful branches that lined the boulevard. Mature trees gave soothing comfort in the summer as they offered calming breezes. The large trees along Rondo Avenue took on double duty. They created cathedral-like arches that shaded people strolling up and down the street. The maples, elms, oaks, and cottonwoods stood as centurion guards protecting the children from fast-moving cars that sometimes flew out of control.

The living historical markers, wide in girth, with gnarled limbs, were planted a hundred years ago because someone had an idea and the hope of turning prairie land into a neighborhood. With a sense of pride, the silent markers call attention to the age and past prosperity of the area. Today, older and younger people walk past the trees, not noticing their stately presence, but caught up in the current world, laughing with and acknowledging each other, walking and moving to unheard music. Unknowingly, they step to the drumming of their past as they enjoy the comfort and shade provided by the trees.

Rondo Avenue moved. The main artery gave life, commitment, and courage to the community. Everything on wheels—bicycles, cars, streetcars, and trucks—used Rondo Avenue. The activity was constant. The energy was intense. Everything and everybody added to the intensity of the neighborhood scene.

Being seen was the main reason to be out. As cars passed by, long and short arms waved greetings to those on foot, to those sitting on steps or stoops, and to those who had found a special place on a porch to sit and view the rich tapestry of life. It was a living portrait that could never be caught on canvas or film. Cars zigzagged from side to side, narrowly missing cyclists and pedestrians. Rondo Avenue accommodated two-way traffic with a streetcar and parking on both sides of the street. Drivers became experts, navigating the narrow path with their expert skills. The sounds and movements of honking horns, shouts, familiar waves, and warm smiles produced and nurtured the neighborhood spirit of a robust community.

Even the laundry hanging in backyards moved with the excitement prompted by spring or summer breezes. Diapers, school dresses, work shirts, and darned socks jiggled back and forth as the wind played with the garments. The wooden clothespins held the corners of the fabric hostage to the rope. The pinning did not stop the frantic dance and the need to move. Faded winter overalls moved as if they wanted to reach the freedom of the street and connect with the neighbors. White sheets and colorful towels welcomed the drying breeze. Well-washed clothing seemed relieved to dangle in the fresh air and wiggle with strong tugs to test the tough line. The clothes, just like their owners, were happy to be released from the cramped quarters of the house, enjoying a few hours of vitalizing sunshine. They flapped with gay abandonment on spring days, doing a freedom dance.

The main artery supplied everything the community needed. The churches stood as cornerstones for the soul of the community. The mix of businesses and residences fostered unity between homeowners and business owners. Everyone worked for the interest of the whole. They collaborated to keep the street clean and the property in good repair. Someone planted a flower garden in front of the grocery store.

Those without transportation didn't have to do without necessities. Delivery drivers brought everyday essentials. The liquor store made deliveries that soothed spirits and buoyed a party up. The local grocery store delivered dry goods. Their trucks added to the movement in the streets. The vegetable man brought summer and fall fruits and vegetables on an overloaded wooden wagon drawn by a friendly horse. Women would dig into their private stash and bring out a dollar or two to buy fresh cobs of corn, green beans, or sweet, juicy peaches.

Insurance agents came to the home and made sure life and burial insurance policies were kept up to date. Families wanted a respectable burial and not a passing-of-the-hat funeral. Parents, who took out additional policies, handed over hard-earned money and precious coins weekly or monthly to ensure a better life for their children.

In the end, Rondo was a stage where a people swayed and whirled to the music of life and death, joy and sorrow, and love for each other.

Winner of 2021 Sidewalk Poetry Contest

(*Untitled*)

DR. ARTIKA R. TYNER

I AM . . . Rondo
and connected to a rich cultural history
of unity, faith, and purpose.
I AM . . . my African roots.
I AM . . . freedom and justice.

CHAPTER 2
INTROSPECTIVE

"The only time I'm pleased with myself is when I'm exhausted and shaking from having written too much."
—*Mabel Seeley, writer and member of the Mystery Writers of America*

"I think I've always wanted to be a writer . . . and used to tell people that I wanted to be a bookkeeper when I grew up—that is until I found out that what I really meant was I wanted to be a librarian or a book artist."
—*David Haynes, African American teacher and writer*

"It is good for one to appreciate that life is now. Whatever it offers, little or much, life is now—this day—this hour—and is probably the only experience of the kind one is to have."
—*Carol Connolly, Saint Paul's poet laureate and columnist literary critic*

present moment morning

MARC ANDERSON

sitting on a worn blue zafu,
thirty years of daily use
urban artist's loft
brick walls 140 years old
oak wood slat floors
same era—
from trees that predate that by a couple hundred years
single source sheng
picked six months ago
from a tree in China—1,100 years old
clay teapot, five years
the water, timeless
and the breath moving in and out, in and out,
not mine—also timeless
animating teeth and bones
and pale blue eyes—sixty-three years now
i'm waiting, like a little boy for the sun,
four and a half billion years shining (give or take a few)
to breach the burial mounds on the east ridge
where ancient spirits have been resting through hundreds of winter
    seasons

My Royal

MICHEL STEVEN KRUG

I carried my Royal down sandstone steps
The terraced Mississippi Bluffs, my arms
Nearly succumbing to the girth of steel,
Sometimes jamming the keys together with

My re-grip so when I finally found a
Grassy patch among the worn and bleached cliffs
The toothy keys were speechless and jammed.
Pried them apart, falling in with a zing.

So satisfying to tap the keys again.
Like playing piano to the river
Whose only response was shore lapping
When ore barges pushed wakes that found land.

After a few stanzas, I smelled a bunched
Towel crammed near the tree line flung by lovers
Abandoning their musk before Saint Paul's
Finest shone a midnight beam on their frisk.

This Royal was my father's. He composed
Business until bequeathed for my poems.
Keys smacked the spool once you found her rhythm,
Sometimes those keys clenched when overeager

Composition inked fingertips that smeared
The poems with age. I regret storing
The Royal in the furnace room where cats
Pounced on the keys and snarled the ribbon

Rendering the Royal incoherent.
During a purge she will be tossed or should
I leave her on a Mississippi patch
Where someone could restore her magic?

Open the world to another young poet.

❧ Winner of 2021
Sidewalk Poetry Contest

La Poesía No Es Lujo

DR. GABRIELA SPEARS-RICO

La poesía no es lujo
para encerrar en un texto

Mi poesía urge
como urge el tiempo
Mi poesía ruge
como ruge el viento

El arte de mis palabras
no tiene precio
Y no está de venta
el sonido de mis versos

Mi poesía es pobre
y aún así te alimento
Mi poesía es pan
para nutrir al pueblo.

Translation from Spanish

Poetry but Not for Leisure

Poetry is not a leisurely
trapping of words on a piece of paper

My poetry urges
like time urges
My poetry howls
like the wind roars

The art of my words
    bears no price
And the sounds of these verses
    are not for sale

My poetry is poor
and even then it feeds you
My poetry is bread
to nurture the people

Where I Hid the Bodies

JORDAN HIRSCH

INSIDE. OUTSIDE.

That's where I hid the bodies. Where else would I put them? Where else would they go?

First, I hid the bodies inside of me. Slowly, slowly; year by year.

My parents talked of diets before I knew what those even were. Junk food wasn't my weakness, just too much of everything else, but meat and potatoes were just as good as hours of basketball and biking.

Mom and my doctor weren't concerned, until Dr. Keys died and the new guy used a new word: obese. Why that word to describe me when there were so many others to choose from?

Like strong?

Coordinated?

Capable?

Every yearly physical, I tiptoed onto the scale, knowing it had gone up but praying the fifty laps I'd run around our yard the day before had undone my lack of "portion control": another new vocab word from doc.

Friends didn't use those words; they just poked my chest to see what boobs felt like, too young to understand that six-year-olds don't have real boobs. My extra body just needed a place to go.

But then my actual boobs joined the party earlier than most of my classmates'. Ashamed to change for gym class, ashamed of hiding my new extra body in some hammock. Though it was nothing but sports bras for years, until my thirteen-year-old body traded spandex uniboob for lacy dividing and conquering for my sister's wedding.

I didn't mind hiding my extra body in high school; I was smart, and I knew it, and I was funny, and I knew it, and I was young and in love with someone who kind of loved me back.

Then that guy broke my heart, and I took my body to college in Minnesota, to bigger and better things.

The freshman fifteen didn't come until my sophomore year when I discovered that the perfect dessert was a full bowl of cereal after every meal. My friends were doing it—why shouldn't I? Not the type of peer pressure I'd been warned about.

So slowly, slowly, I added more body to myself.

Then Mom died, and I was grief incarnate, carried around by the pound.

Adding forty was a piece of cake—or rather, stress-filled spoonfuls of peanut butter.

Adding twenty was different. It was gradual and full of healing. A boy liked me. I liked him back. We were happy.

We got married.

And in my comfort, joy, and acceptance, I added forty more.

Then one day, Dad had yet another heart episode, and I panicked. Three bodies wouldn't lead to a long, happy life. Three bodies would encourage my genetic time bombs to detonate: cancer, heart disease, diabetes.

I put my bodies outside beneath a two-mile stretch of sidewalk in Highland Park. Again and again I traversed that concrete, until I ran out of room. Then I hid them under three miles, under four. Did neighbors know what bodies I hid as I circled our block?

Five miles, six miles led my spree to Lake Phalen, and they put a medal around my neck after my second lap. Was I the best at hiding bodies? Or maybe I was a war hero, doing battle with myself for twelve laps around Como Lake.

It wasn't just outside. It was a game of Clue—me in the kitchen with the paring knife. I trimmed fat off meat; I roasted up veggies. And I ate.

Unlike previous attempts where hiding bodies meant 700 calories a day, trying to starve them away, I fed, nourished, and healed my body.

And you know what it told me then?

Just because you're happy with extra bodies, with extra bites of food, with hours on the couch, doesn't mean you won't be happy without those things.

Loving yourself doesn't depend on one body or three.

Loving yourself is choosing not to hide the bodies anymore.

The Difficulties of Low Standards

AMANDA BOYLE

MY ARMS WERE LAID UPON the cold wooden table, a number two lead pencil was beside a college-ruled notebook. This was the dreaded daily routine for my second-grade self, consistently put on the spot to write detailed summaries about the only book that my mother ever purchased. What else could I expect from her? The pressure of the system that was built against her was drowning her. She was trying her best to shield me of any prejudice that would be placed against me in my future educational career. Reading and writing was the one thing that would target me and many other minority students for the rest of the time we spent in any school located in the United States. From questioning our ability to read and write, then judging it harshly; to finally randomly placing us in English as a second language courses to make sure that being fluent in other languages does not affect our ability to speak the preferred language in the United States.

The way that teachers address problems in a child's reading or writing work is the foundation that the rest of their educational career is built upon. That is proven through the rest of the time that I continue to spend in any space that helps my pursuit of higher education.

Indigo blue, the smell of dry-erase markers filled my nose. I was confused, wondering why this red-haired teacher specifically pulled me out of the classroom. She handed me a pile of laminated note-cards, obviously used before as they had been completely worn out. She asked me to read the words that were scribbled on them with what looked like a thick black Sharpie pen. I read until the pile of twenty was reduced to zero; an emotion was written on her face that younger me assumed to be surprise. My mother was a caramel tone and my father absent—how did I manage at such a young age to beat the statistics? Then reality was highlighted, her face stormed my memory for as long as I could remember. My first-grade self became aware that the minimum expectation for everyone else was my average, their failing score was my passing.

I wonder at times if she had not reacted in such a way toward a score that defined my reading level, would I have been more success-ful? That thought will stand for the rest of my life.

A few years went by and I realized that I no longer had to put effort into school. I stuffed my pink homework sheets right next to my yellow spelling list, between where my desk met the vent, pro-testing against what I believed at that time to be a useless activity. The standards were low, hard to not meet, I never crunched on time to finish anything. I felt a level of calm and serenity that I do not know if I will be able to achieve again. Yet I wonder how I would have viewed my first years of school if the issue had been addressed differently.

Through these experiences I learned that being critical of my work, whether that be reading scores or pieces of writing that is okay in certain situations, I should allow myself to have some free-dom with both. The standards that were placed for me have been beat, easy enough when my mother was told that I would finish high school reading at a ninth- or tenth-grade reading level. The way that teachers address issues in a child's reading or writing work is predominant for how they view the rest of their time pursuing any type of education. If every child is given the self-worth and confi-dence in the beginning, they will be more successful through the rest of their educational career.

Unexpected Seasons or the Luck of the Draw

CATHERINE BOEBEL GROTENHUIS

FEBRUARY 16, 2017

HERE IT IS, February in Minnesota, and no less than sixty degrees outside. Global warming concerns aside, after four months of merciless winter, being out-of-doors in such warmth feels akin to winning the lottery. Maybe better.

Saint Paul's streets are astir with pedestrians unexpectedly emerged from hibernation—blinking in the blinding sunshine, stretching legs unaccustomed to walking unfettered on ice-free sidewalks, and ravenous for sights and experiences beyond the confines of winter's lairs. Faces that, only yesterday, turned downward to ensure safe footing are, today, upturned in greeting. "Nice weather, isn't it?" (Minnesotan for "We just hit the f-ing jackpot!")

Unlike many passersby, *my* kind doesn't hibernate, but chooses instead to conquer winter with the hearty constitutional of a daily four-mile walk, exposing a person to the elements year-round. Thus, February generally finds me bundled to the max as I forge through subfreezing temps, ice, and snow. Yet, incredulously, today I've left the house without this season's parka. Nor chunky Smartwools laced into hiking boots (with hefty soles sufficient to scale the Alps). Nor my lumberjack-checked cap with earflaps (a nod to Elmer Fudd and keeping winter lighthearted). Today, mere sweatpants, a loose-fitted T-shirt, a hoodie, and my blue sneakers suffice.

One mile from home and I'm grinning; walking feels like flying. Overnight, I've lost five pounds and will easily shave close to ten minutes off my time—a complete fitness overhaul. What a difference a change of season makes.

As I stride past the bustling shops on Grand Avenue, gusts of fresh air cascade down my now unzipped jacket, delighting every inch of exposed skin over which they pass. Every epidermal cell awakens, as if from a slumber of its own; each nerve fiber exclaims at the long-forgotten, and utterly delectable, sensation of the wind's caresses. No polite nods or mumbling about nice weather from these quarters. My neck, shoulders, and collarbone cry out with the fervor of a four-time winner at a southern VFW. "Bingo! Holy moly! Praise the Lord and shout Hallelujah!"

Breasts, nipples, and belly quiver with ardent abandon as the temperate breezes brush . . .

Stricken, I jolt to a stop. Nipples? Belly? WTF?

My eyes dart down to my chest, half-certain I will see that I am standing half-naked in the middle of Grand Avenue. Once . . . then once again, I scrutinize myself to ascertain that I am, indeed, fully clothed.

I am, of course. Just so much less so that I *feel* half-naked.

With a laugh, I continue on my way. Amused at thinking I could possibly have left the house undressed. And suddenly, blatantly, mindful that the day may lie ahead (not for many years, but *someday*) when, heading out for my morning walk and (pausing mid-reach to grasp the doorknob) I will carefully ponder the large-print words scrawled on paper that's been painstakingly taped to the doorframe, precisely at eye-level:

"MOM! TURN OFF THE STOVETOP BURNERS AND BE SURE THAT YOU HAVE ON A SHIRT AND PANTS BEFORE YOU LEAVE THE HOUSE! —XOXOXO"

Yes, that day may come. It's all in the luck of the draw.

And today?

February in Saint Paul, Minnesota, is one lucky place to be.

Etiquette for My Funeral

ISADORA GRUYE

Mark my words.
Whenever my time comes,
it'll be far sooner
than I would have liked.
Let them chitter on about
my uselessness,
my wasteofspaceness
my should haves,
my didn'ts,
but also remind them
I drank from a garden hose
that was always on full blast.

And I think it would be beautiful
if you could somehow
get all my minutiae
to gather around me and join hands:
that teddy bear I bought myself at twenty-nine.
Bukowski's recipe for egg salad that I printed out
and kept tucked in my day planner.
All the striped knee-highs from my sock drawer.
The principal balance of my mortgage.
Tubes of Chapstick squirreled away in my glove compartment.
My collection of rocks that look like Bill Murray.
The library card I spent months trying to get.
The tomato plants I tried to grow on the fire escape.
Have them all hold hands around my grave
until there is a circle twenty-five miles in diameter
of all the worthless shit I ever wasted time on.

Recollections in Flame

LARRY D. McKENZIE ("SLIM")

THERE I WAS rubbing hands and stomping feet trying to generate some kind of warmth in my backyard. No matter how much I jumped up and down, the cold was still winning.

Now one of the things that I really enjoy is a big old blazing fire, particularly in the winter. Days as a Boy Scout coming through, I guess. A longtime compadre of mine years ago cut down a huge oak tree. I ended up with some serious-size chunks. With one remaining hunk after a few good fires under my belt, it was the perfect scenario to unleash my inner pyro. Now, kids, don't practice this at home. I rolled this huge chunk of oak over to the edge of the pit. I had busted my hump one summer digging and lining it with concrete. Half the stump hung over the side. The more it would burn through the night, the more I would feed the hunger.

As I drizzled some gas on leftover branches and that stump, I began to reminisce of days gone by. The peaks and valleys, the many subtle shades within the bold varied hues that color a person's life. Times which shape the body of our landscapes. Lines that define our relationships, friends and lovers that have crossed and stabbed me in the back. Lovers that I have crossed and disappointed. I tossed a lit book of matches into the pit. The frostbitten air instantly ignited into a flashing cloud of flame.

It was one of those midsummer nights, calm just before the storm. I was living on the first floor of the fourplex building on the corner of Oxford and Iglehart. I could see the Jimmy Lee Recreation Center, then just beyond that was Central High School. Chilling out in the living room, it was about 11 p.m. Suddenly there was this intense pressure and urge to step outdoors. So I stepped outside and from my viewpoint the high school was in direct sight. The sky was voided in black; no stars, no moon, just an absence. Then it came bared, like a lead weight. I witnessed a lightning bolt that lit up the dark, just one badass, thick bolt. The tremendous thunder was immediate, so powerful it shook the windows. Mind you, I get startled like anyone else at loud, unexpected noises. Yet in this instance, there was a feeling of being connected to something grander, majestic. Then nothing, not another bolt. Not even one raindrop to grace the hour. Only silence to send me back indoors.

Then there's the birth of my firstborn. The sounds of "son" to my ears seemed odd. Me a dad, never thought it would happen in a million years but internally grateful to be one. Midway Hospital on the second of June '87 was when he blessed his mom and me with his presence. The heat that early summer was thermometer cracking.

The thing I remember the most after his birth was the extended stay. He needed, oddly enough, to spend time under the heat lamps. To this day he is still a pretty cool character. They moved the three of us into a wing of the old but functional hospital. It was like stepping back through time. Lots of pastel tiles, rounded edges, chrome, and Art Deco styling. We had the whole wing to ourselves and ordered a pizza. We threw back the windows and let the summer breeze in. The temp had dropped to a reasonable degree. On the first night being left by ourselves as a family, everything felt fresh and good.

When I looked up from my thoughts, the fire had gorged its way into the center core of the stomp. It began shooting its way up through the oak like a chimney stack. A single dark-blue flame hissed and burned. Bits of orange sort of flowed and flickered about the edges of the towering blaze. The warmth it offered soothed the angry cold.

A passel of recollections came easier under the comfort of the fire. We've all, at some point, been touched by something uniquely profound. These recollections left their extraordinary footprints on the red carpet of my Saint Paul experience.

Dream Sequence #3

SEE MORE PERSPECTIVE

All is silent. A silence as certain and distant as peace.

There is a friend in my home who is not a friend. This should be my old compa Jorge who would often visit, stay the night, rap, and make art with me on the sides of buildings and overpasses and banks.

Not ever on anything independently owned, nothing without a purpose or a genuine question, and nothing without art. Jorge laughs like fireworks look and there's always fun around the corner of his smirk.

A friend is here, but it is not my friend.

It is disguised

in a disgusting mask of flesh

swollen and puffy

and it doesn't fit its real face.

A darkness peering from black eyes and

I'm trying to keep it cool,

casually taking in information of this rotten,

bloated presence over my shoulder.

I cannot face it.

When I look back I am terrified by what I feel

and my words fall like dead flies brushed off a windowsill.

I slowly return to the task at hand.

It doesn't move a fraction, a petrified vision of malice.

I'm washing the dishes . . .

eyes in my back like thorns,

the most intense leer like the
soft

tap

of a spider's legs

that want in.

This day is weeks and months and these years just a sunny
afternoon outside. I come and go, I'm busy and I'm only
stopping in to leave. This *unfriend* living in my home, with
my family, my mother, my younger sister, and our pets

There is a tepid but constant squalor in the downstairs

. . . is this what happens to a dream deferred?

I maneuver carefully through the by-products of this spirit's
wretched intent

with casual talismans . . . masks and drums and décor.

I am cleaning and organizing.

Washing the dishes again.

Behind me,

a grotesquerie of intent, a masterpiece of some sick artist who's left
his greatest work to stand and watch . . . me.

I tell him he can't stay. He'll be needing to leave immediately.

I continue working on the basement's floors (you),

shelves (cannot),

cracks (stay),

closets, (you *will* leave)   and the walls . . . the walls suddenly
stand out.

I'm talking with my mom and kissing her forehead and just then
I'm under her bedroom in the downstairs, right underneath
where she lies and I'm hanging a mask. I know it is gone. There
is a slow silence like the most beautiful new snow

There is light here and I awake.

Senses

LEILANI ANDREWS

When you look outside of your window, what do you see? Is it a gray sky or a blue one? Maybe it's one of those perfect skies that mix blues, oranges, pinks, and purples on the big canvas in the sky.

When you're walking outside in the city, what do you hear? Young children playing outside with shrieks of excitement? Maybe you hear birds singing a song that only they can perfect.

When you're stepping out of a vehicle, what do you feel? Is it a cold rush of air that forces you to get inside as quickly as possible? Maybe it's warm enough that your skin isn't pushing out beads of sweat and you feel wrapped up in a comfortable blanket of warmth.

When you're thinking to yourself, what do you know? Do you wonder when your favorite type of day is going to be coming along? Maybe you embrace every day as a favorite because it's in a city where no day is ever the same but always familiar.

CHAPTER 3

FAIR & FOUL WEATHER

"I love the rainy day, the quiet room, the books, the pictures, and
the glowing fire."
—*Arthur Upson, nineteenth-century poet*

"The guy who takes a chance, who walks the fine line between the
known and unknown, who is unafraid of failure, will succeed."
—*Gordon Parks, photographer, writer, and screenwriter*

"Writing is something warm and dependable to snuggle up to when
everything else is in flux. It's a little secret that you carry with you
in public—the knowledge that you alone have the ability to escape
to a wonderland where you can make anything happen."
—*Judy Delton, prolific children's book writer*

Lowertown Haiku

COLLEEN CASEY

amid brick buildings,
artists' lofts, craft breweries,
bat hits ball—and CRACK!

Weather Girl

BETH L. VOIGT

WITH A FURROWED BROW, my nine-year-old daughter watched the Weather Channel. The forecast was for sunshine in the morning and sleet in the afternoon. She looked at me, started to say, "What should I . . ." but then sighed and turned back to the television, imploring it to tell her the proper attire for biking down Lexington to school in the morning, biking home after what was sure to be a sweaty gym class, and staying comfortable in between.

She knew I wouldn't be of much help.

While I certainly wanted my children to be safe in Saint Paul's frigid temperatures and comfortable in its blistering heat, I didn't offer them much more advice than "wear a jacket" or "maybe shorts." She knew I adhered to the philosophy, taught to me by my father so many years ago, "Don't let the weather control you."

When I was her age, I rode my bike down Hillcrest Avenue's bumpy street in the rain, raced outside barefoot to the alley in the snow when it was my turn to take out the trash, and wore embroidered jeans in the heat of summer because I thought they looked cool when I walked down Ford Parkway to my softball practice.

She, in contrast, rode her bike in a T-shirt and shorts, but stuffed her windbreaker into her bike basket just in case the weather suddenly changed. She wore rainboots outdoors but carried her tennis shoes with her in case the sidewalks dried up. She wore jeans in summer but would readily discard them for the shorts she had on underneath if it got too hot for her.

As I grew into adolescence and eventually adulthood, I interpreted my dad's advice as: there is no need to listen to the weather reports. Why bother knowing what the weather will be if I'd find out as soon as I walked out the door?

That philosophy didn't sit well with my daughter, however.

But I just couldn't seem to break my habit of ignoring the weather.

For years, I didn't own a raincoat or an umbrella. I owned a pair of winter boots but rarely put them on because of the inconvenience of having to take them off.

This, admittedly, has caused me a few problems. I recently got caught in a downpour walking a short distance from my car to a daylong meeting where I sat until my clothing air-dried. On more than one occasion, I've walked out to my car after work on the outskirts of Saint Paul to find it buried in snow. Without a hat or boots or sometimes only flimsy ninety-nine-cent emergency knit gloves my daughter stored in the glove compartment, I paid the price, brushing inches of thick, wet snow off my windshield, sometimes with the sleeve of my coat.

By the time she was nine, my daughter had almost given up on asking me about the weather.

I'd occasionally pass her as she checked out the Weather Channel and say, "Grandpa says, 'You're in charge of making it a good day or a bad day, not the weather.' Wear what makes you happy." She ignored me.

At ten, she scanned the week's weather forecast. Once she even asked me about purchasing the *Farmers' Almanac*.

By age eleven, she was a weather geek, walking out the door with layers of clothing to add or shed at a moment's notice. With shoes on her feet and boots in her backpack. With an extra hat or scarf that she was willing to loan me if she felt I was unprepared for the weather.

While my father may have had a different meaning in mind, with his advice not to let the weather control us, we added our own slant to it. I chose to ignore it most often, and she chose to prepare for it. Either way, we weren't letting it control us.

March Snow

JAMES SILAS ROGERS

Newscasters work hard to frighten us:
highway spinouts, clogged snowblowers,
bundled up strangers pushing our cars.

Yet, even the meteorologists
who earnestly declare that today's storm
is shaping up as an unholy mess

understand that it won't last.
Coming inside, we shrug off the snow
and laugh. The willow in the backyard

and the bare apple branches are flocked
again, a minute after you shake them.
But the mailman made a joke, and

sure enough, brought seed catalogs.
We've finally reached the crumbling
days of winter, letting go

our icebound caution. We know
snow uncloaking from an apple branch
anticipates the petal-fall to come.

April Snow

LOREN NIEMI

Outside the half light
The sound of plows clearing
A parking lot, beeping back,
Scraping forth, then the clang
Of the garbage truck working
Its regular schedule,

The snowblower works the sidewalk
The wind works the window
Curtains flutter where the window leaks,
Miles Davis's *Nefertiti* is the soundtrack,
And if all is not right with the world
This moment is right with me.

April in Minnesota

ANNETTE GAGLIARDI

I see them everywhere, slicing
the soft earth, slipping their speared tips
skyward—stretching their spikes
of green and purple.

They emerge in regiments, in battalions,
fighting for space with other newly forming
species. The war is waged through rain
and sun, through day and night; with all

their might, they surge upward
tilling the soil with their appearance;
surfacing, and then unfurling
shining new leaves, as they rise.

And I want to throw my hands
upward and thank the sun—shout
out to the world, when I realize,
"The Hostas are coming!"
"The Hostas are coming!"

Hip Hop Hope

CATHERINE AYANO NIXON

Midsummer calls
Says stroll to the park
And bring along that
Bag of art
Drawn by the sounds
Beat of the drum
Boom of the bass
Singer step stomping
Along
Reaching out to the crowd
Hips swaying
Calling back aloud
Graffiti rainbow spraying
Children run playing
See me
Hop across the water
Leaping stone to stone
Hope watching
I lose myself
In lines of light and
Melody moves of many
Gathered here
Creating heaven for a day
Oh
Make it stay

Autumn Afternoon on Blair Avenue

LISA HIGGS

I've never known patience like the squirrel,
fence-top as the dog's eyelids lower.

I've never been still like the grass
whose job is to grow and be cut and grow.

Autumn seeps through links, yard
by yard, a raccoon foraging to morning;

the schoolyard wraps fog to its throat.
How close sleep can be to grace,

young girl at my breast. I thought
I'd never fit anywhere, belong anywhere,

like fall to its leaves changing
on a cool night always in the dark.

If I sat here long enough, was still
long enough, I'm certain I could see time.

Minnesota Snowfall

KAREN SANDBERG

Ed bundles up, trudges out to clear the driveway.
Supper smells soon fill the house.
Flakes drift heavy messages to oaks,
gnarled arms spelling January poems to sky.
Wind lifts its wings,
hawk of the prairie,
each motion sending drifts
from the roof.
Late afternoon
wanders
into the west
enticing night bloom of cold stars.

Miracle at the Auditorium

LOUIS DiSANTO

WHEN I FIRST BECAME a runny-nosed little rink rat in the early 1950s, the facilities at East View playground on Saint Paul's East Side consisted of an old caboose, a potbelly stove, and a custodian named Mike, who kept the place toasty warm and dispensed words of wisdom and encouragement to kids like me, who fell down a lot trying to master the fine art of skating and shooting a hockey puck at the same time.

Money being tight (a gourmet meal at my house consisted of fried baloney on Wonder Bread and Kool-Aid), it was necessary to improvise when it came to equipment. I used *Life* magazines for shin guards, kept my stick together with nails, and stuffed socks into the oversized skates a cousin gave me. My patched and frayed jacket wasn't exactly a Montreal Canadiens jersey, but it provided a reasonable buffer against the relentless cold.

Despite being teased about my ragtag appearance and weak ankles, it was a passionate love of hockey that helped me to persevere and work hard until I became a regular participant in pickup games and shoveling the ice. And yes, I eventually did get genuine Gordie Howe shin guards, skates that fit, and stronger ankles.

It was during these formative years that I began hearing stories about the State High School Hockey Tournament and the epic battles between the large metro schools, especially Saint Paul Johnson, and the powerful teams from the frozen hinterlands of northern Minnesota. Fascinated by this wildly popular sports event, I dreamed of one day attending the tournament at the Saint Paul Auditorium.

That dream finally came true on February 24, 1961. According to the *Saint Paul Dispatch*, a few tickets were still available for Friday's semifinal games. So my dad, Joe, my brother Tom, and I headed downtown, hoping to witness the highly anticipated showdowns between four of the state's top teams.

After a quick bite at the nearby White Castle, we ran over to the Auditorium expecting to waltz right in, only to find a lobby so packed that we could barely squeeze through the doors.

When the ticket windows opened, there was a tsunami of desperate fans that pushed Tom and me away from Dad and against the back wall. As we did a contortion act to keep from getting crushed, it became painfully obvious that there was a better chance of spotting Elvis than getting in to see those games.

Then, through this utter chaos, I saw my dad holding up three fingers and passing money to a young man he knew stationed next to a ticket booth. Incredibly, this man proceeded to pass back three precious tickets, which drew the stares of many envious eyes, not to mention some jealous sneers.

We were absolutely dumbfounded! If sportscaster Al Michaels had been there, I think he would have shouted, "Do you believe in miracles? Yes!" long before he made that famous declaration after the U.S. men's hockey team stunned the Soviet Union at the 1980 Winter Olympics.

Considering the pandemonium in that lobby, the scarcity of tickets, and the odds of having a friend in the right place, "miracle" is the only way to describe how we went from agony to ecstasy.

That was just the beginning of an unforgettable experience. In two of the best games I ever saw, Roseau beat North Saint Paul 4-3 in triple overtime, and South Saint Paul, led by Doug Woog, edged Duluth East 2-1. The crowd of over 8,000 was going absolutely wild, shaking the venerable old Auditorium from its smoke-filled rafters to its very foundation. And we savored every beautiful moment.

We stayed for a while after the games, letting our blood pressure return to normal. Following all the excitement and raw emotions (I remember some girls from North Saint Paul who couldn't stop crying), the quiet, half-darkened arena suddenly took on this dreamy, surreal aura that I found mesmerizing.

Sleep came grudgingly that night. My ears were ringing and I kept playing those games and how we got the tickets over and over in my mind.

Tom and I spent much of Saturday roaming the neighborhood like minstrels, regaling everyone with our amazing story, which gave us a small measure of fame. And the story got more colorful and dramatic each time we told it.

We watched the championship game that evening on our grainy thirteen-inch black-and-white Zenith, the first time the tournament was televised. Roseau blanked South Saint Paul 1-0 in another heart-stopping contest that had us yelling our lungs out as we ate our baloney sandwiches. But it sure wasn't the same as being there.

My brothers Joe (1969) and Mike (1973) both had the privilege and thrill of playing in the tournament for Saint Paul Harding. One of Mike's teammates was Paul Holmgren, who went on to play ten seasons in the NHL for the Philadelphia Flyers and Minnesota North Stars, and also served as president of the Flyers. In September 2021, Paul was inducted into the U.S. Hockey Hall of Fame.

Over the years, I've seen many memorable games in this nationally renowned Minnesota tradition, which began in 1945 and, except for a few years, has always been held in Saint Paul. But none can quite match the pure magic of that February night in 1961, and the "miracle at the Auditorium."

CHAPTER 4

FAMILY MATTERS

"How did the writing bug bite me? Maybe this way. My father was first a high school teacher, then a librarian. . . . My mother is a born teller of folktales. So I started life with a book in my hand and well-said words in my ear."
—*Mabel Seeley, mystery writer*

"I don't want to knock it. But I wrote television to support my family. If I'd had my druthers, I would have written novels . . . I didn't want to write *Wild Wild West* or *Bonanza* particularly, and yet I needed it."
—*Norman Katkov, writer*

"To love is simply to allow another to be, live, grow, expand, become. An appreciation that demands and expects nothing in return."
—*Kate Millett, writer*

Čhaŋté Wadítaka

TANAǦIDAŊ TO WIŊ | TARA PERRON

Thokáta wičhóičhaǧe kiŋ,
Tókhetu thaŋíŋ šni kiŋháŋ dé abdéza; Wačhéuŋničičhiyapi,
Waúŋničičhipi,
Uŋníčidowaŋpi,
Wóuŋničižupi,
Nakúŋ wóuŋničihdakapi!
Čhaŋté waníditake!
Nakáȟ, nihákab naúŋžiŋpi!

Translation from Dakota Language

Heart Warriors

Grandchildren of the future:
When times are uncertain please know this.
We prayed for you,
we danced for you,
we sang for you,
we planted seeds for you,
and we spoke for you!
Your heart is strong!
And now, we stand behind you!

Welcome to The Lexington

PATSY KAHMANN

OCTOBER 1968

I CLEARLY REMEMBER the first time I crossed the river to Saint Paul. Dad had sent a cab to my dorm so I could join him at The Lexington, where they were already celebrating. It was my eighteenth birthday.

I was a new student at the University of Minnesota, a small-town kid trying to navigate a stony city. Our hometown was a hundred miles and an era away from this ritzy restaurant.

Dad had discovered it while traveling to the State Law Library in Saint Paul. He had been researching a project, and a lawyer agreed to help.

The doorman welcomed me while trying to take my coat, but I didn't understand the coat check protocol and pushed my hands deeper in my pockets. He pointed to a booth in the back. There was Dad waving a long piece of paper at me. My older brother Karl was there, and Mom, and the lawyer I had heard about.

"Katy, bar the door," Dad hollered across the lounge. My name isn't Katy, but Dad wasn't referring to me. It was a favorite expression of his, one he would shout out when something remarkable happened.

I could tell this was Dad's kind of place—mahogany paneling offset with soft gaslights, a long robust bar, and "the best damn martini in 500 miles." Dad had been a salesman before the accident. His job had taken him to upscale restaurants in Chicago and New York.

Something about this tableau in the corner booth made me feel at home. I took off my coat. Dad placed the legal-size papers in front of me, pointing to my name in the guardian section. My parents were designating *me* the guardian of my ten younger siblings.

It was their last will and testament, an unusual birthday present for a college freshman. With the stroke of a pen I became an adult.

Sort of. I couldn't vote or drink alcohol, but I could legally parent a house of kids if called upon.

You see, five years earlier a brutal car crash had sent my parents to the hospital and my siblings and me to separate foster homes. There were twelve of us kids, the oldest fourteen, the youngest a baby. Our mom was not expected to survive the night. Dad's back was broken.

Month after agonizing month we lived with strangers, separated from each other. They called it a miracle when Mom recovered enough to leave the hospital and Dad found a way to bring us all home. "Katy, bar the door," Dad shouted that first night of our reunion. "Nobody's getting past me again. I promise."

But the reunion felt fragile. Our parents were now considered disabled, and caseworkers would come to the door of our home checking, monitoring, judging. Dad's obsession to keep his promise kept him up at night. He needed to formalize a will and nominate a guardian. But who could be trusted to keep twelve children together? In the middle of a sleepless night, he found his answer.

Minnesota State Statute, Section 517.02. There it was: Children were considered minors until age twenty-one, with a curious exception. A girl could get married at eighteen without her parents' permission.

Dad pounded out this theory on his trusty Royal typewriter with its temperamental keys. It followed logically, Dad typed, if a girl could get married, she could be a parent . . . so why not a guardian? My brother Karl was older by a year, but in 1968 the law wouldn't bend for him. He was about to be drafted into the Army but legally was still a minor.

Dad raised a toast while the lawyer leaned over and whispered to me, "You're a loophole adult and it might get challenged in court, but I promise to fight for you."

I held the document up to the gaslight and stared at my name. "Sleep well tonight, Dad. No one's getting past us again."

The Guitar Lesson

REGAN BYRNE PALMER

THE LACK OF A PIANO in his home embarrassed my dad. Without a piano, his children couldn't practice and you couldn't take lessons unless you practiced. He and my mom might have scraped together the money for lessons, but never for an actual piano. He frequently referenced our lack of musical aptitude but never did much to rectify the situation. My friends were tortured by piano lessons, so I never cared.

His friends put together a band at his favorite bar, where he went after work to socialize and avoid his family. Suddenly he couldn't be heard over the trumpet and clarinet, his sanctuary snatched away by some sheet music. To fit in, he had to learn to play something, preferably something portable. You can't lug around a piano, but guitars come with handled cases. Although he couldn't play, he bought a used guitar from Schmitt Music on Sixth and Cedar and signed up for lessons. "I don't know" and "I need help" were phrases he loathed to utter. But with a child in tow, he could ask someone to teach her and learn alongside.

I must have been lurking near the front door, avoiding homework, staving off the sadness that gripped me on those first gloomy days of fall with my mom on the night shift, when he left for his first lesson, because he dragged me along. Downtown Saint Paul at night in 1975 was an unknown to me. We took the bus during the day to go to the dentist or peer through the windows of Frank Murphy and Gokey's. The evening when I was in the fifth grade, a welcome light leaked out through the rain-smeared windows of Schmitt Music as my dad swung his new old guitar case between us and we walked into the store together. In one corner, a ring of folding chairs shared music stands. A practice guitar, superior to the one my dad bought for himself, became mine for the lesson. We sat side by side.

As our fellow students arrived, my dad joked and teased about attending his daughter's lesson, fooling only himself. I took lessons as a child—Sokol Gymnastics, Andáhazy ballet, softball at the park. He'd drop me off, leave, and was usually late to pick me up. He was not at Schmitt for me, he was there for himself, at least on the first day.

The instructor introduced himself and I imagine we shared our names. I was by far the youngest person there. My dad had finagled me into an adult class. The instructor tuned his guitar. He picked and plucked, one foul note followed by a crystal-clear note in a pattern that became the background music for the remainder of my school days as my dad tuned his guitar in this manner from that day onward. Then, without any preamble, the instructor played "I Can See Clearly Now" while knocking out the percussion on the wood of his guitar. The sound was rich, full, reverberating through the wood of the guitar I held in my own hands. I was determined to learn to play that song, even if I never played anything else.

Because I had the better guitar, during that first lesson my Cs were sharper, crisper, my Gs full throated. If my dad was irritated by my beginner's luck, he never showed it. When we left the lesson, something had changed between us, although we never spoke of it. We went weekly until he was no longer a beginner and could fake it with his friends. He played the guitar for the rest of his life, until he grew too sick to hold it.

On fall evenings, the welcome glow of home calls me inside to create; calls me to try something new. It is in those moments I remember Schmitt Music and how it gave me time with my dad, no matter the pretense.

Our Reflections

JUDY HAWKINSON

Sometimes birds break their wings when they fly into windows.
Why did he do that? she asks.
I reply, maybe he saw trees.

Look. It's us. I point at our reflection and I am pointing back.
She looks at herself in the window.
She's wearing her pink baseball hat, an orange T-shirt,
and a red tutu.
Trees are behind us.

There we are, I say, and I wave to her.

And if we were trees, we would look like trees in the window.
We stand and stare and think about
looking like trees.

But the bird was also lucky—
because he could fly.

Sometimes the bird would fly high in the sky
and the wind would lift him
and he would let the wind push him
and he could even dance.

The bird lived an urgent and glorious life.

Would you like to dance? I ask.
Her reflection nods at mine.
I lean over and pick her up
and we dance in circles.

She throws her head back and laughs at the sky
and the clouds
and the cottonwood balls
that rain down on us.

And for that moment
we, too, are living urgent and glorious lives.

The bird stands up, flaps his wings, and flies away.

Salut Américain

CASEY GORDON

MY BROTHER IS ACROSS FROM ME at a restaurant called Salut Bar Américain, adjacent to an Anthropologie and across the street from a J.Crew in a neighborhood where I imagine everyone is nice and tends their lawns and has at least one prime time television show that they watch as a family, and as much as I hate to admit it, the place has got "good yoo-hoo," as an old friend of mine would say. Good yoo-hoo is weighted heavily in my daily equation, which takes a familiar breakfast, a brisk walk to work in comfortable shoes, a respectable amount of wine in the evening hours, and shimmies them all together into a nice elixir that I use to feel balanced. A restaurant with good yoo-hoo is not to be taken for granted, even if the neighborhood itself is a bit of a bore.

My brother is across from me. He wears a device on his head that sends energy fields into his brain to slow the cancer cells, to frustrate them into cell death. The cells cannot separate, as cancer cells so badly yearn to do, and they die, according to the informational video I watched. Cell death, they called it, which felt brutal, direct, aggressive—a nice foil for this pleasant, hospitable neighborhood, this expensive restaurant and its delicious wild mushroom short rib pappardelle.

"How was your meeting with your advisor?" I ask.

The waiter drops bread at the table, a French baguette with whipped butter, red salt, and marinated olives. The baguette used to be free, but they've started charging $2.95. We both have lemonades, it is hot out, and our table has a red and white checkered tablecloth.

"Oh fine," he says. "They're letting me take a leave of absence, put my dissertation on hold, then after a semester we'll meet again and see if I want to pick it up. I think I could write a bit here or there. Just to have something to do."

We don't talk about his cancer. When I first moved home, my mom and I tried to talk about it, but it was too hard. Somehow we were never on the same page. One of us in the dark place, the place where the cancer was terminal because solemn doctors and internet statistics told us so; the other of us miraculously steeped in gratitude and hope. Our talks would devolve into tearful arguments— our entire worlds had been flipped upside down, only the arguments enduring, familiar. So we stopped talking, and only communicated how we felt through subtext, which is incredibly Minnesotan.

"That would be great, Hunter. It's nice to have things to do." I am clunky, awkward. I don't know how much we're supposed to talk about the future.

"Did I tell you I bought a plane ticket?" I ask. "To New York. I'm going to go for the Fourth."

"No. That sounds fun," he says.

"Yeah, for sure." My voice doesn't even sound like my own. "I'm excited."

A year ago, before the doctors found the tumor, I had flown home from New York and we had gone up to Duluth with his wife and kids, my mom and sister, and stayed on Lake Superior. It was June, but only about fifty degrees or so on the north shore. We took the kids to see the lighthouse, went for pie at a place called Betty's, and one evening we stayed up late drinking and tapping out songs with our feet to see if anyone could guess the tune. We called the game Toe Jams and laughed as we wove epic tales about becoming famous because of our musical feet, that we would have to insure them, that we could be rich and live in mansions and ride power chairs everywhere because our feet had become too valuable to walk on. It was a duel of the absurd versus the absurd-er that we fought well into the night, and we laughed so hard we probably cried, though I don't recall exactly.

"Fourth of July in New York. That'll be nice," he says.

"Yeah, I think so," I say.

"Maybe I'll have to go with you next year," he says.

I rip off a chunk of the baguette and dip in into the whipped butter with red salt. The yoo-hoo is good, the energy fields slow the splitting of the cells, somewhere nearby an old man pricks himself in the finger while doing yard work and puts it in his mouth to make the blood stop.

"Next year," I say. "Next year it is."

Heating Season

NORITA DITTBERNER-JAX

Early October and the furnace kicks in,
earlier than it did when you lived
on Cook Street, alone, retired,
sweaters keeping you warm,

buying diabetes strips with money
that should have bought groceries.
All your economies come back to me
in the autumn chill.

Your life made me sad sometimes,
you, a single mom, seven kids,
until I was a single mom and then
I learned from you. Here's the revelation:

Sister, I think you lived the way
you wanted to, husbanding your resources.
You lay aside enough money to pay
your nursing home bills, and when

you died there was money for your children.
Sometimes I picked you up from work
and dropped you off at the bank,
and you never said a word

about salting away money, not a burden,
but pride in taking care of yourself
with enough left for the word that conjures
spacious lawns and porticoes:

by damn, you left an ESTATE.

Sitting in Silence

ALIA JERAJ

WHEN I WAS FOURTEEN my dad moved into a house off of Fairview and Grand. My mom and I would go visit periodically. She'd play the house's old piano and adjust the lamps in my dad's bedroom. When it was nice out, we'd all go on a walk around the neighborhood, looking at the fall leaves or admiring people's gardens. I learned to adjust my pace, slowing down to match my dad's hesitant steps on the uneven sidewalk. My mom and I would leave before dinner, sometimes stopping to eat pho or falafel on our way home.

I remember texting my tenth-grade boyfriend. "My mom and I are going to my dad's house today," I typed into my Razr flip phone. "And, FYI, my parents aren't divorced—my dad just has Alzheimer's and lives in a group home." I don't remember how he responded.

My dad spent two years in a home called Rakhma Joy. He was the youngest of his seven roommates, brought together by dementia. His room was on the bottom floor, just outside the living room. It was probably a repurposed sunroom, surrounded by windows on three sides. The room was small—just large enough for a single bed, a chest for his clothes, and a chair. My mom would fuss about the cold getting in through the old windowsills and whether there was enough light during the winter.

My time at Rakhma was mostly spent in silence. At fourteen, my patience was limited. Being around the sick and older adults terrified me. I didn't know how to reconcile that stage of human existence with mine of youth, health, and naivete. I hadn't yet collected tools to even acknowledge my emotions, much less process or express them. I didn't yet speak the languages we use when we aren't able to use our words.

So I would sit in silence in the single chair in my dad's bedroom, texting anyone who would respond. I'd walk just far enough ahead of my parents. I'd find solace in conversations with other families visiting their loved ones, or with Comfort, one of the women who cared for my dad.

In time, my mom was able to bring my dad back to our home, with the help of Comfort and other nurses and volunteers who became family. He died three years later, surrounded by family. I've often found myself back in that neighborhood—drinking bubble tea after senior prom, participating in a staff training for my first full-time job, and singing at Khyber Pass. One day, maybe I'll be ready to go back to Rakhma—volunteer my time and visit with the current residents, have conversations in languages no one can study, and take leisurely walks through the neighborhood. For now, when I find myself near Fairview and Grand, I simply take a moment to sit in silence and remember my dad.

Biking in November

CARLA HAGEN

WHEN I RIDE MY BICYCLE in November down Summit Avenue in Saint Paul, I think of my Grandma Anna, who emigrated from Norway in the early years of the twentieth century. She would have shrieked had I even suggested riding in temperatures like the 20s and 30s Fahrenheit, snow or no snow. *Gud i himmelen! God in heaven! You will get sick for sure! You will die!* Yet I know she walked—or rode a horse, if she was lucky—for miles in the subzero air of Lake of the Woods County on the Canadian border of Minnesota, where she and my grandfather homesteaded. Outfitted for the cold, face framed by black wool, I fancy I look like her: shawl wrapped tight around her head, long wool skirts brushing the snow. I thank her for a sturdy body built close to the ground and made to move.

I take myself back to her house in the woods—washbasin in the kitchen, pump outside, outhouse down a winding path. At her round oak table, I draw or write as wind scours spruce branches, rattles windows, and drives the mink she raises into a large, furry cluster in their pen. She sits across from me using a magnifying glass to read her Norwegian newspaper. The only other sound is the crackle of wood in the oil-barrel stove that heats this part of the house. Smells of baking bread and Castile soap. Sometimes I think if I could go back, even for five minutes, this world would fall into place again, like a town that emerges when you stop shaking a snow globe. But I now know those times were never innocent; as a child, I ignored their complexity. And yet I long for a blue woolen shawl wrapped around me, the scent of my grandmother's rye bread. For someone to yell at me for riding my bike in November.

Mama Has Passed On

DEBRA STONE

theater: *noun,* a construction or edifice for dramatic performances

Here comes:
Aunty J with her good hair now the color of a silver fox swooped over one eye like Veronica Lake swings it as she enters like Beyoncé. Mrs. M with her Blackglama mink coat a legend in her time gives J the evil eye.
  This is an Episcopalian funeral no drama here.
  That is to say, there won't be any fighting, whooping, hollering, or fallout crying here.
As
Johnny Mathis sings, Chances Are & moments later Sarah Vaughan contradicts Johnny Mathis with a song no one remembers the name of. Mama's friends chatter & laugh, reminisce about old Northside, Rondo & eat the catered food piled on the rented tables—my sister & I career women too busy to cook. This is what our Mama wanted.

theft: *noun,* an act of larceny; stolen

January
One week before my birthday, Mama died. My birthday always stolen; three weeks after Christmas everyone's broke. Wait until spring Mama would say, you'll get your present then.

You're so self-centered said sister.
At the age of three sister was lost at the Northside parade, the policeman asked her, what's your mama's name? Mama she said.

Sitting by Lake Bemidji, sketching the Willow tree, leaves smelled like grass and the Mallard Duck with his emerald crown bobbed in the water while waves lapped on the shore. The Willow tree, its thick branches with bark like varicose veins stretched over the water. I remembered, on a rope swing we jumped into Bassett Creek, the Willow branch broke. Sister hit the water; the branch fell on her head. A drowning person makes no sound. I jumped in, grabbed her by her hair. Dragged her to the bank. She sat up and shivered and I gave her my towel. She never told Mama.

theism: *noun*, belief in the existence of a god or gods

In the underworld Mama refuses Hades & his wife Persephone. She was never one to obey. Just ask her husband. Dad said she made Father Brown delete "obey" from their marriage vows.
Scandalous in 1950.

They were scandalous: A North Minneapolis boy from the Sumner Projects marries a bougie Saint Paul girl from Rondo Avenue; places buried in cement now. He'd ride the University Avenue streetcar with Fanny Farmer Fudge and roses, their courtship. Daddy Joseph said bring my girl home by 10 p.m. young man.
Daddy Joseph was not playing.

Octogenarian friends, women a few men, struggle in deep snow, bone rattling bitter cold with walkers & canes through doors still tough not defeated by death bid Mama farewell. They no longer drive.
Their children bring them or the Metro Mobility bus.

cremate: *verb*, reduce to ash

Cremated remains are pulverized bone, the body reduced to 3-7 pounds. I didn't want this writing to be about Mama dying of cancer infecting her lymph nodes, the breast, then the entire body in five years.

Things Mama disliked:
My 1970s Angela Davis Afro.

I would "borrow" her lingerie, sweaters & sneak them back in the drawer.
Rolling my eyes.
Sassiness.

She didn't harbor many dislikes.

When I lived in Senegal for a three-month sabbatical she called me every Sunday at 8 p.m. The phone would ring & the Senegalese operator would say with a pronounced French accent, it's your Mama, then remind me after we hung up—don't forget your Mama will call you next Sunday. Mama had never traveled outside of the United States.

Sometimes I listen to her recorded voice message on my cell phone, she says: hello, it's mama . . . as if I don't know.

She rode on the back of Daddy's motorcycle cross-country for two months in the summer of 1994. They were still scandalous.
She took care of all the family dogs and cried with us when they died.
She considered herself a working woman: mother, housewife, bookkeeper.
She read everything.
She was my champion.
In anger, I once said, I'd never be like you. But I am like you, I look like you, sound like you, I'm tempered like you.
It's your revenge you knew I'd be like you.

Her last night was a good one with the family surrounding her bed to say farewell. At 2 a.m. the night nurse called to say, your mama has passed. I knew this before she called. Mama's perfume floated into my bedroom & with a light touch to my cheek, said she was leaving.

This didn't happen; I dreamed it.

Dad's Grip

GEORGE SLADE

THAT CURLED HAND GUIDED MINE through jigsaw puzzles and crosswords. Dealt out hearts, gin rummy, cribbage, Oh Hell, MacMillan's Awful, and some still-mystifying game called Russian Bank. Stymied me, repeatedly, at backgammon. Exemplified how to carry a shotgun safely in upland thickets and fire it effectively at elusive timberdoodle, quail, and partridge, and how to shoot bottles bobbing in Lake Superior, way down below the Big House and Birch Bay bluffs. How to make a winter's supply of firewood with a log-splitting machine the day after Thanksgiving.

All that is beyond his hands' capacity now because his brain has lost the map. The puzzle pieces and words are irrevocably scrambled. Boggle and so many of these games reflecting Dad's love for language and strategies are now mine to convey to young people in my life—in my own fashion, always knowing who gave them to me; who continues to hand me things every day.

"Just getting rid of a stray eyebrow," Mom says. Dad tolerates it like a seven-year-old getting his hair pushed back on his forehead. "So everyone can see your handsome face." Her reality has always been so intertwined with his. Now, when his reality is, as far as we can see, a psychedelic wandering through terra incognita, she is at a loss. To put it mildly.

He was, though, clearly tuned to her wavelength. From where I was sitting, if not from where she was. The challenge is being with him where he is, however inscrutable it seems to us outsiders. He reached out to her several times during lunch yesterday, placing his arm solicitously on her back and regarding her with what passes for delight.

He didn't eat as much of his pulled pork sandwich as she would've liked ("you're getting so skinny, Richard"—followed shortly by "I'm sure your son will be willing to help finish it"—which is true, and the reason I only ordered toast and fruit). He shook his head after each bite she fed him, though he did enjoy his coffee with, get this, cream and sugar.

The setting: a casual fall gathering at Jack and Kirsten's house. My local family is extensive; an invite instantly yields several dozen warm souls. Dad shuffled in and settled on the couch with his sister. Cousins, in-laws, and grandkids swirled around in the graceful, unconscious way they do. Dad crossed his legs, propped his cane across his lap, wore his bright Saint Paul Saints cap, and gazed at it all, a still point enmeshed in family. The best place.

This one area of his room, within reach of the foot of his bed, is rife with touchstones; the rest of the space is relatively without character. There's a Lake Superior shore scape, a glamour shot of a long-haired dachshund, and a solid, extremely old-fashioned engraved nameplate that graced the desk of a businessman known as G. R. who strongly resembled the distinguished gentleman in the portrait. Though the desk embellishment is wildly anachronistic here, Dad recognizes himself in that picture—a good sign. He extends his brass-handled wood cane toward the adjoining photo of Mom. He knows her, too, but is mostly wordless in his regard for "that one," that person with whom he shares six-plus decades of marriage but from whom he is now inexplicably, irrevocably estranged.

In my hand

MIRIAM WEINSTEIN

Today, from the top shelf of my closet, I retrieve a large box
of photos. Years compress and expand. Photos ten and fifteen
years old mingle with photos taken twenty-five years ago

of a family vacation. Cobblestone streets, and a street market
in Mexico, a plain wooden playground, my daughter swinging
from monkey bars. Much like the iPhone video her husband

sent last week, their seven-year-old daughter, her legs
swinging to fill the frame, proudly shimmies closer
to the camera. A video runs in my head—

my granddaughter as a toddler sways from a jungle gym,
then I see images of her at four and seven years old moving
along bars. I continue to shuffle through piles of photos,

one comes into focus. My daughter at the state capitol,
her first choice a tour of this majestic building on her sixth
birthday. Hand in mine, I remember how she tilted

her head to take in details of artwork on the ceiling. How
she called her name, again and again, delight on her face
as she listened to the echo of her voice under the round dome.

Home after our tour, she slept curled in the recliner, her legs
in lavender tights stretched over the arm, her feet wrapped
in boot slippers.   Now, here—in my hand,

a photo pulled from a haphazard heap—my daughter asleep
exactly as I remember. Photos, some in plastic and paper
envelopes, some held together with rubber bands.

A medley of memories in my mind as we dash to the swing
set and, for a moment, are all six years old, pumping
higher and higher our legs

extend   in a race to touch the sky.

A Poem for Oliver

WENDY BROWN-BAEZ

Rocking next to the Christmas
tree, the child in my arms sleeps.
Colored lights slide over his face, our peace
as reverent as if we knelt in church.

Let his breath come even and soft, let him
fidget, held beyond waking or dreams.
Let his brightness never fade, let him be wild
as the stars slung across the sky.

Let him reap the fruits of love. In his tiny hand
sugar plums leave a sticky sweet.
I think carefully on this world he has
entered. The TV tells me all

I need to know of pain and grief: shattered homes
from last month's storm, gunshots ringing
out in bloodied streets, foreclosure notices point at
where a family once lived, moved on to some other sorrow.

Snuggled safe, this child knows
neither hunger nor fear. The worst that has
happened is a tumble, a pinched thumb, a brother
shutting the door.

I intend to keep it that way but we can't keep him
from life. His heart will be broken—he will lose
and be lost, cry with rage and pity. But
I pray it is not too soon,

and does not last any longer than he can bear.

CHAPTER 5
TRUTH TELLING

"Being an activist artist is not a sprint. It is a marathon. Artists need to plan and strategize and build their forces for the larger battles to come, to fight from strength not weakness."
—*David Mura, Japanese American writer, editor, educator, and mentor*

"The stories that were being told about African Americans at that time didn't have the breadth or richness that I knew the culture to be capable of. . . . I wanted a place where those more complicated portrayals of African Americans could be told."
—*Lou Bellamy, founder of the Penumbra Theatre, stage director, actor, producer, and educator*

"But believe me, there is beauty in it still. Truth. The light of freshness is buried in us and in every moment we breathe. It is there. Sometimes we are so encrusted, so rotted over with misery, bad situations, that we can't see it. Feel it. But it is there."
—*Alexs D. Pate, African American writer, editor, educator, and mentor*

Stones

JULIA KLATT SINGER

Each word a stone.
We can build a wall
or a
path
to
each
other.

Tim Tekach and Jocelyn Hagen have turned this poem into a song.

Bdote (*ba-doe-tay*)

THOMAS LaBLANC

Bdote,
it is where the rivers meet,
it was that,
before
this
place
was called
Fort Snelling
this
place used
to take us Dakota
away from here.
Bdote,
it was here
before
Minnesota
it is, where the water comes together,
it will remain
Bdote,
forever,
no matter,
what we say
or do!
Bdote!
Bdote!

Minnesota Nice

TY CHAPMAN

At six years old, me and mine moved cross country,
all our worldly things tight packed in a Ford Contour.
Our black and white cat mewed gently beside me
as the Texan breeze blew through open windows.

I played Gameboy as the streetlights allowed,
not knowing fully why we fled. We odysseyed
upstream, a single craft in a fleet of others, making port
at whichever motel we could sneak a pet inside.

We went by freeway for fear of being the next mess
to litter country roads—to be bound and battered
in small town south. But the north is no stranger
to country roads or making messes, just attentive
to cleaning up postmortem. We couldn't know

how snowbanks can obfuscate
brutality, how traditions spread
from sea to shining sea, how
histories can never be left behind.

At fifteen, I watched a cop shove a child
down concrete school steps, his body flailing
between impacts. His skull battered
to fragments. Crimson rivering
down a well-ironed shirt.

The child, beaten
into my memory, was bound
and ferried away. He was made

an example, to every Black
kid with the gall to ask "Why?
What did I do, officer? Get your
hands off of me, officer. You're
hurting me, officer. I can't breathe,
officer." A reminder,
some traditions spread
coast to coast. A reminder
they can never be unmade.

In the north, neighbors hide
behind niceties and dial 9-1-1
if one too many negroes occupy space.
If we ask too many questions or
carry on too loudly. Here they despise
confrontation, and call well-armed
militias to lynch on their behalf.
Here, Black kids learn
to watch over shoulders.
To look for red and blue lights,
because they know our nation's colors
are synonymous with death.

They know some traditions are old as
shipping routes; that there is no port
or corner of the country
where the same rules don't apply.

They know a legion is eager to take them,
that their headline is already penned.
How this nation aches to break them.

How this history is never left behind.

Under the Dome of Dominion

NORA MURPHY

O White Georgia Marble
Keeper of our State's
damaging ways and means,
how do we awake to the
suffering your makers deny?

Not everything we validate
is visible. The eyes, the heart, even
the stories we've been filled
with cannot be paraded as
Evidence A before your Courts.

Yet eyes give us the world to
wonder, the loon's red piercing eyes,
her reflection on still pond. Heart gives us
galaxies of feelings, leaping like your
golden horses, scorched like grief.

Stories make meaning of the world.
With each breath, we swallow syllables
so fine we cannot see their filaments of
hierarchy, separation, and greed, nor the
invisible net they weave.

Nestled under your dome of dominion,
do you cling to this pernicious web of
tall tales because you believe them,
or simply because you are afraid
to let go?

Labels

MARYAM MARNE ZAFAR

They only had to look on him
and they knew what he was
They didn't even have to hear him speak
or peep his last name
They knew all about him
They knew his origin
his nature
and his destination
and they would always tag him
with a prefix
or a suffix
till finally
they just buried him alive

Naturally enough it came to this
with all those Indian acts they kept passing

He only had to look on them
and he knew what they were

Sometimes some of them
would even offer a hand
in friendship
but he knew better
He could see right through
things like that
All you had to do was read the signs
and the signs were written
all over them
signs he never put there

The labels we wear are
far more important than truth
Truth has nothing to do with anything
because

The fact was
he was not white
They were
and that's all that mattered

Mourning Paper

ARLETA LITTLE

Today's front page features the dead. The unnamed
marshals who killed Winston Smith at the top of a parking ramp
in Minneapolis's Uptown in June
will not be charged.

Guns were present. Guns were pointed. Guns were fired.
God bless the dead. *

In a flanking article, the Crow Wing County attorney
says it doesn't matter who drew first
(or that this Black man is no longer
with us as a result of the encounter).

Guns were present. Guns were pointed. Guns were fired.
God bless the dead. *

At center page, a reverend and city council person, both Black
men, stand with heads bowed in prayer outside the Seventh Street
    Truck Park
after fourteen people were injured and one died in a mass shooting
    on Sunday.
Marquisha Wiley, age twenty-seven, was killed in the crossfire.

Guns were present. Guns, with poor aim and disdain for life, were
    fired.
God bless the dead. *

At the bottom of the page, an article announces a new U.S. postage
    stamp
celebrating Día De Los Muertos. Forever stickers feature sugar
    skulls
surrounded by marigolds and candles. The living welcome back
the souls of the dead but there is no mention of how they died.

Pour out some liquor.
God bless the dead. *

Tell Me, Mariposa
(For the monarch butterflies in our lives)

DAVID MENDEZ

Tell me, mariposa
That what our people say about you is real

Tell me, mariposa
That you are the realization of resistencia
In the natural world

Tell me, mariposa
That your journey
And struggles
Is our own story

Tell me, mariposa
That you are the ancestors among the marigolds

Tell me, mariposa
That our instruments and songs
Give you strength to cross the continent

Tell me, mariposa
That our footsteps shake the colonial strongholds
Over our sacred earth
That every blood and teardrop
Will make the path less painful
For those who follow

Tell me, mariposa
That you carry the names
Of our missing loved ones
Long after we used our last breath calling them

Tell me, mariposa
That we are healing
Because we chose to exist

Tell me, mariposa
That we are forgiven
For our human frailty
Our cruelty, our arrogance
Our every transgression

Tell me, mariposa
That our scars
Will not carry over to the spirit world
Or pass to the next generation

Tell me, mariposa
That our loved ones fulfilled their journey
To the Creator's arms

Tell me, mariposa
That we are still loved by the spirits
That they hear our prayers

Tell me, mariposa
That our movement continues
That you carry our resistance

Tell me, mariposa
That our danza and our drums
Bring medicine to our people

Tell me, mariposa
That our languages
Are still spoken

Tell me, mariposa
That we no longer carry
The curse of traumas
That we carry blessings
Along with new hope

Tell me, mariposa
The words of your sacred footprints
So that we may find our way to you

Tell me
That we the descendants
Coming back once more
Beyond all storms
Still thrive

Connecting

REBECCA NELSON

THIS MEMORY is one of the first experiences of historical trauma that I remember, before I knew exactly what historical trauma was. It happened at a powwow in Granite Falls one summer when I was vending for an Indian taco food truck. I had picked up the gig on Craigslist with a woman from Saint Paul. We met at Magnolia's on Payne Avenue and hit it off perfectly, and we followed the powwow trail all summer long. I loved it.

This experience affected me profoundly and makes me sad and tear up every time I remember it. I was at the stand early; it was my job at that time to set up our stand before we opened. The sun was shining very brightly, as it does only during the early morning, and it was already warm, just bordering on hot. It was going to get blistering hot later on, but at this moment it was still okay. I loved this part of the day because I was able to sit peacefully and comfortably by myself under the tent before the hustle and bustle began, and just soak in all the activity. I listened to the drums and the songs as the flags were raised and the emcee welcomed the new day and described the songs being sung to honor various events and people.

The morning ceremony began by honoring the thirty-eight Dakota warriors who were executed in Mankato, reading their names out loud in both English and Dakota. I don't know why, but tears began to well up in my eyes. A feeling of despair and overwhelming sadness slowly crept over me. I knew about the Dakota thirty-eight, but I hadn't really understood what had happened and what it meant to the Dakota people, my people. I just felt very sad. Having been adopted as an infant by a Scandinavian family, I have limited knowledge of my culture, and this was one of my first powwows.

The last song of the morning began with the introduction of a letter written by a Vietnam veteran who wanted to honor a friend of his. The emcee read the veteran's letter out loud, his voice carrying across the powwow grounds, broadcasting through the speakers to the campgrounds farther away. The letter told the story of how this veteran had met his friend in boot camp and, both being Indigenous, they bonded and became good friends. They went to Vietnam together and fought in several battles side by side and at one point were the only two to survive a particularly deadly battle—deadly because of faulty equipment. I remember the emcee's voice as he was reading the letter, as being matter-of-fact, with no emotion. And yet the words were making me cry. The letter continued as the writer said the two lost touch after the war, his buddy returning to the Pine Ridge reservation and he himself returning to Oklahoma. He thought often of his friend and eventually began to attend powwows in South Dakota in and around Pine Ridge. He spent many summers searching, hoping to catch a glimpse of that familiar face in the crowds. As the years passed, he began to search cemeteries, eventually finding what he was looking for. He knew it was his friend, as the saying on the gravestone was one he had heard his friend say often. It read, "I know I'm going to heaven because I've already been to hell."

It took me an hour to regain my composure after hearing this. Why no one else was crying, I don't know. I figured out later that even though I was adopted, I still felt the historical trauma that came with learning more about my Indigenous world.

Finding Shelter

LISA KASTE

MY NAME IS Agaamishkode namadabiikwe—the woman across the fire. When we are at a fire, I receive messages from our ancestors. I am from White Earth Nation.

My daughter and I moved to Saint Paul from Duluth on August 1, 2010, fleeing domestic violence. During my daughter's entire kindergarten year, we lived at a domestic violence shelter before getting housing. After moving around for a few years, we finally found a home in the Summit/University area, where we currently live. I recall after moving out of the shelter, I started looking for jobs. One of my goals became giving back to the community that helped me while I was in the shelter. Eventually I got a job at St. Stephen's, where I currently work as a homeless advocate. It was not easy in the beginning. I didn't have transportation, so getting up at 4 a.m. to get to work was a state of mind. I would go to work in the dark and come home in the dark. No matter how tired I was, I would remind myself, "At least I get to go home and be safe."

Since moving out of the shelter in 2011, I have worked myself off Section 8 housing assistance. That was so scary. It was 2019 and I had two full-time jobs. I got the letter from housing with my assistance end date. All I could think was, "Yes, I did it!" It encouraged me to help others do the same. I still work two jobs; one is still at St. Stephen's, the other as a program supervisor at Avivo. I supervise staff at our tiny home village for the homeless. We have one hundred tiny homes.

Homelessness is such a big issue. It doesn't go away, and it can't be covered up. There are waiting lists for shelters here. If they say, "Sorry," what are you going to do? You and your kids stay with people until you can't anymore, then you're just outside in encampments that are continually being torn down. There's no reason why anyone, especially children, should be living outside or in a vehicle.

A lot of the Native American services in the Twin Cities are in

Minneapolis, like Kateri, Little Earth, and the American Indian Center. In Saint Paul, our primary source of help is the American Indian Family Center, which is a godsend. I don't know what I would've done without them. As a Native American trying to access some of those services, I always had an issue with transportation—it was not fun getting on the bus to go to Minneapolis every day, especially in the winter.

So I've decided to work on opening up a Native American homeless shelter in Saint Paul.

Shelters are usually divided between men's shelters, women's shelters, and singles. My vision is to open a family shelter. This is especially important to me, because the term "family" in Native American culture is very broad. Family can be the grandma taking care of six grandkids, or cousins living together. Any combination of family members is considered family.

All homeless people are fighting for the same services, and when those services are not available, it gets to be very emotionally draining. My shelter will include job counseling services, licensed alcohol and drug counseling treatment services, mental health services, and, of course, housing advocacy on site. That way, people living at the shelter won't have to get on a bus to access these resources. Having a reliable job is a really big thing. How are you going to get housing if you don't have a job?

I am the woman across the fire. I know my ancestors don't want us suffering.

Elders are a part of every decision I make. When an elder speaks, you listen. My elder told me that it's my turn now to help my people—someday my elders will become ancestors. And someday, I will become an elder.

Having shelter is a way to healing. It's hard to heal when you're outside and it's cold or it's hot. It's a basic right everybody should have. I need to get this shelter up because it will provide a new start. . . . It's someone's life; it's someone's death if it doesn't happen.

My name is Agaamishkode namadabiikwe—the woman across the fire.

I Know Poverty

LEQUETTA DIGGS

I KNOW POVERTY. My earliest memories take me to a room with concrete floors and stone walls. The room was storage space for a rundown restaurant that was nestled on the edge of a poverty-stricken neighborhood on the east side of Wichita, Kansas. My mother, my infant sister, and I moved there to join my father, who had found a job working at a meat packing plant. Back then, makeshift housing was not unusual for migrating African American families. There were no hotels or rentals available to us, so we took shelter wherever we could until more desirable housing could be found. The room was dirty and had a moldy odor I will always remember.

Before long, my parents found a small house and we moved. My grandmother lived next door to us on one side of the house and a railroad ran along the other side. The house was a step up for us; we felt lucky.

The country was at war. We were entering World War II. I remember watching trains go by, filled with young soldiers. We knew they were facing the unknown, like the rest of us.

Commodities were rationed—sugar, butter, nylon hose. People did what they could to get by. We had a garden, and we raised chickens. The gardens and the chickens were our main source of food. To feed the chickens, we swept grain remnants from empty box cars that were unloaded at the stockyards. Preserving and canning food was essential, because there was very little that you could purchase on demand, even if you had the money. Prosperity to us was having enough food to feed our family and to keep a roof over our heads.

We bought very few things that were new. We were poor, but we didn't call it that. And our poverty had little effect on the way we felt about ourselves and our neighbors. We were constantly reminded of our virtues, our potential, our talents, and our responsibility to ourselves and our community. We could not have asked for a more caring environment. We knew we were loved.

After working for more than thirty-five years as a psychiatric nurse practitioner, I retired and decided to devote my newfound free time to something different. I joined Experience Corps and was trained to be a tutor in the public school system. I was assigned to Maxfield Elementary School, which sits on a frontage road on the north side of I-94.

I see poverty in Saint Paul today. Many children come to school tired, hungry, poorly dressed, unkempt, defensive, and angry. They are more interested in survival than they are in learning. They have very little faith in themselves, and even less faith in their community. They are weary, and they worry about things children should never have to worry about.

They are afraid. What are they afraid of? They fear loss, put-downs, embarrassment, violence, and uncertainty. They are surrounded by an external world that has very low expectations of them, and they know it.

From my work through Experience Corps, I know a school in Saint Paul where one-third of the children on any given day are homeless or facing homelessness, where the incidence of asthma is the highest in the city, where their last meal of the day is the snack that they receive just before school is out in the afternoon, and where kids fall asleep during lessons because they had trouble sleeping at the shelter the night before.

Recently, I congratulated a little girl for her academic achievement by telling her she could grow up to be anything she wanted to be. She asked me, "Like what?" When I answered with a list of career choices, she began to cry. I asked her why she was crying, and she replied, "Nobody ever told me I could be anything."

Her poverty and the poverty I experienced as a child are different. They are different because my community and my school were constant reminders of my strength, my ability to survive, to become anything I wanted to be. They are different because when I was growing up, we never considered ourselves to be in the wrong place. We were always home.

Inequalities of Life

MIN SOE SAN

Translation from Burmese

While your friend's daughters are attending schools
Umbrellas in hand

Our little daughter sells flowers
as a vendor on the road.

While you are cleaning fish and prawns

Your friend is strumming
a musical instrument called saung,
humming along songs.

While your friend's wife is sitting down
meditating

I am, your wife, selling Bein–mont (food) on the ground.

While your mom, my in-law, fries batter on the roadside

Your friend's family happily went
on a journey of pilgrimage.

While your friend's daughter is attending
a ceremony for graduation,

our daughter is helping with
Tha-Na-Kha paste grinding.

Dear Eternal God
Who loves everyone,
Please correct the inequalities of life
with your almighty power.

I no longer wish for this life
Where there are no smiles or happiness
. . . within me.

Not Long Ago

MEE YANG

NOT LONG AGO, a girl was born to the Yang family. Paker was child number two of five. She graduated from Como High School. She worked at a bank through college and became a manager. She lived at home and graduated from college with no debt. She dated throughout college and met people from different ethnic backgrounds. Her pride in her own culture and language grew as she admired her friends' ability to communicate pride for their unique cultures. That was when Paker decided she wanted to marry a Hmong man who also appreciated their colorful culture. Life coasted by as she waited for the right man to show up in her life.

Paker volunteered in the Hmong community and attended events with her parents, which included Americanized events such as weddings, funerals, fundraisers, and traditional Hmong ceremonies that celebrated newborns, those returning from long hospital stays, and the elderly. She had a master's degree and was working on her PhD. She did not have a boyfriend. At the events she regularly attended on weekends around the Twin Cities, her *aunties* often asked her when she will marry.

"Paker, you have to marry one day," an aunt told her while they were preparing a meal at a traditional funeral. Traditional Hmong funerals can last up to three days and three nights. "You are a grown woman now; you can't rely on your parents forever. You have to marry so that others will respect you."

"I work, I have my own house, and I pay my own bills," she responded cheerfully. She was introverted as a child but learned to become more outspoken during college.

"Paker, how old are you? Forty years old?" the aunt asked, not looking up at her. Other aunties around the kitchen, also wrapped in aprons, scoffed.

"No, auntie, I just turned thirty this year." Paker felt her pride leak out of her chest beneath her apron and spill onto the floor.

"Oh, your cousin Mai is thirty. She has five kids already." The aunt volunteered what she thought was useful information.

"My cousin Mai, who recently divorced? You can't be comparing us to each other? We have such different life experiences," Paker stated, not looking up at this woman she no longer wanted to call aunt, the stench of the garlic they were peeling engulfing her. The already small funeral home kitchen encroached into their conversation, the long rectangular metal table where they were preparing vegetables and herbs seemed to distance itself.

"Don't just wait for a good man to find you. You have to go find one. Women like your cousin Mai are on the market again. This is her second time on the market searching for a man. So what if she has five kids? She's also respectful and kind. She's reserved and doesn't talk back like you."

Paker's mind came to a full stop. "I'm not in the market to compete with my cousin or women like my cousin for a man." She took her apron off. "I am in the market to find someone who loves me for who I am. A Hmong woman's value should not be based on how compliant she is to a man. Maybe I won't marry a Hmong man. Maybe I'll marry a white man. Maybe I'll marry a doctor. Maybe I'll marry a high school dropout." She placed her apron down on the table, ready to leave. "I came to help prepare food for a funeral and pay my last respects. I didn't come to advocate for single Hmong women. I didn't come to be compared. I am leaving. And now that I am leaving, you will have to work harder to prepare food for this funeral." Paker picked up what was left of her dignity and left the kitchen.

At her core, she still wanted to marry a Hmong man who would understand all of this.

The Wall

TERRANCE HOBSON II

A wall that I have over-
come is being who I am,
and coming from where
I'm from. Some
people just wouldn't
understand, that in America
it's tough being a Black man.
I have seen friends and family killed
by a gun. Anger and
frustration tempted me
to pick up one. But I think to myself,
will things ever
change with so many people
thinking of doing
the same? Other folks
judge me by the color
of my skin, but they don't
understand the situation
that I'm in. Want to go back and get
my education. Don't want to
sell drugs 'cause if you get caught
they'll give you more time than
a rapist. Tried to get a
job but the managers
are racist. They think that I
won't work hard because
I'm Black, when in reality
it's only a diploma that
I lack. So I jump off
the porch to hang with

the thugs, out here on
the block trying to sell
drugs. A lot of their
stories are the same as
mine, just young black
men trying to survive. To
many others this route
may seem dumb, but
to be honest, this is the
norm where I come from.
I don't want to be like the rest,
I know I'm destined for more.
People say it's hard getting rich,
but it seems harder being poor.
Now I have a decision to make,
do I change my life for the better
or do I keep putting it at stake?
I decided to get my diploma
even though it's late.
I've had so many people
doubt me, I think it's time
to show them that I'm great.

CHAPTER 6
HEART & HEARTACHE

"We must have writers who participate in everything that mankind does and in all its aspirations. We must have writers who believe nothing is distant and far."
—*Meridel LeSueur, activist and writer*

"The writing of books is not easy . . . there must be reliance upon the deeper sources of consciousness, from which the best writing comes to assure anything really worthwhile."
—*Cornelia Cannon, author of* Red Rust

"I discovered one way to get the pain out of me was to write. I wrote and I wrote and I wrote."
—*Darina Siv, Cambodian American activist and writer*

What's Yours to Love

HEIDI BARR

Be reminded
that pebbles, raindrops,
moss, grassy fields, old high bridges,
sidewalks that act as homes, foamy
lattes at your favorite café, a wave
to your neighbor each morning
on the way to work, robins, orange
dahlias blooming, feral cats, urban farms,
protests, peaceful police, Black lives, Checkerboard
Pizza, stately oaks standing watch near crumbling
houses, hidden waterfalls, sandstone bluffs,
long-legged spiders, the person next to you
on the light rail who hasn't showered in weeks,
domed cathedrals, albino squirrels, inmates
who write daily letters to small sons,
children who wake up singing, snow
gently falling on glassy water
in spring—be reminded
all of this, collected,
is yours to love.

Summer Ice Cream

JOSHUA PRESTON

It is not their best date
but it is the life they wanted,

licking clean
the dreams of summer

from tiny, red spoons.

Sweater on the Hill

HEIDI FETTIG PARTON

I am West Side.
  I am hippy chic.
    I am divorced.
      I am single mom.
     You are unattached.
    You are button-up executive.
  You are Ramsey Hill townhome.
You are evenings at the bars on Grand.

In winter, spring, summer, and fall,
  I drive over the High Bridge to find you
    as we dabble in each other, as we pretend
     we are not the other's future.
    When winter comes again,
  I sit by your fire drinking tea and eating
chocolate-covered graham crackers
from your morning run to Starbucks.

"Back soon," you say on your way into the office.
  I enter your closet of crisply pressed shirts,
    spaced at perfect one-inch intervals, to
      find what I need so I can tread Ramsey
      Street in your too-large sweater,
    silently enumerating all the reasons I do
  not fit your orderly closet sort of life.
I do not see your car pass by me on the hill.

Six years into our marriage,
  you write to me on a card:

I am driving home to my carefully
contained and well-appointed life
when I see my sweater
traveling down the hill
on the back of the girl
I have come to love.
This is the moment
when I know that I know.

You say you are not a poet; my love,
some bridges are unwittingly crossed.

I don't know what slows your heart

ELIZABETH TANNEN

     or whether there are ever enough bike paths in Saint Paul
                               to map the news.
The world hemorrhages
           daily.

Beside love, lives science
                 green painted toes
                      mirrors and webs
    of affection that bisect
              our cities like interstates.

I gather dust like a forgotten species of plant,
                  syncopate my attention
                     to your body's
        particular theories
              and blood.

I thought of us when I made
        eye contact with the alley.

Inventoried yesterday's meals
        beside today's loose ambitions.

I heard a metaphor for northbound traffic
           but you'll only understand it
               when walking west.

Listen: if this poem is a prism, every street must spell
             one tint of light.

Sharing Saint Paul

JAMES ZIMMERMAN

I VISITED Amore Coffee one morning just to get my final paper completed for class. I couldn't work on it at home; too many kids distracting me. I entered the café and approached the counter to order lunch.

And that's when I saw him. Over there—to the right, sitting at a long table. And it wasn't just him, it was his wife, and his two little daughters. And one other lady, too. Judging from his necktie and their dresses—and the fact that it was Saturday morning—it was clear they were taking a break from their door-to-door proselytizing work.

My heart quickened. I turned away, back toward the counter, wondering if he saw me, worried that we'd make eye contact. There—not twenty feet away from me—was one of my best friends. I hadn't spoken with him in years. He shuns me now, a position he had made very clear the time we passed each other in Crosby Park. I had waved but he had steeled his glance toward the path ahead.

Still, I gathered my food and purposely sat at a table with a direct line of sight to him. I made busy opening my backpack, my notebook, my laptop.

I attempted to progress on my paper but was far more interested in my former friend. For fifteen minutes we shared the café, furtively stealing skewed glances. Once, I looked him straight on. He was turned, attending to his younger daughter, and I knew he could scarcely detect that my eyes were raised from my laptop's screen.

And then they rose to leave. Buttoning their long coats, wiping the children's faces, collecting their trash. The women left first—out the side door immediately to my left—with the girls in tow. My friend lingered, struggling with a button on his coat. Then he detoured to the trash bin.

He paused at the door. *What was he doing? Bracing himself for the cold, perhaps?* Still fiddling with his coat buttons, he turned toward me. *Is he going to say something? Why doesn't he just say my name?* But he didn't. *Why? Was he waiting for me to make the first move? Should I fully turn, look him straight in the eyes with the biggest smile I can muster, and say, "It's good to see you"? Or maybe "You have a beautiful family"? Or simply, "Hello, Tim"?*

But I didn't. I couldn't. The seconds moved excruciatingly slowly, but I couldn't force myself to turn, to look, to speak. I did not know if I was mad, or nervous, or unsure. Probably all three. He opened the door and, submitting to the winter weather, stepped outside.

I dimmed my screen until it was completely dark, then adjusted its angle until it served as a makeshift mirror. Via the reflection, I watched the group climb into his van. Not sure what my purpose was—likely a combination of stalling on my homework and considering that I might have passed up my last chance to speak once more with my friend, however fleetingly.

Or maybe I was worried about the rejection. Or rather, the re-rejection. He'd been shunning me for a decade now. Doing what he thought was right, and dubbing it love.

Because, really, every shunning is a reminder of the life I left behind, a former religion with conditional love and an exit that offers no closure. And every shunning is a reminder of all the family and friends lost. For both of us.

After ensuring his daughters were buckled, he got in the driver's seat, closed the door, and drove away. I sat there for a long moment, contemplating the reflection. We were still sharing Saint Paul, but we might as well have been in two different cities on opposite sides of the globe.

Near the Corner of Summit and Lexington

MARGARET HASSE

for Jim Moore

You know that time in spring
        when old-fashioned street lamps
        begin their gradual dawning
        at dusk,

that time before lightbulbs grow into small suns
        caught in cages, when it seems
        all other walkers on the boulevard
        have gone home

to set their tables
        or close their windows
        to the chill stirring
        in new grass.

Car traffic suddenly stills.
        You alone get to cross to the median,
        an island where lilac bushes
        gather

like fugitive rain clouds
        white, purple, and blue, where
        branches hold up fragrant torches
        drawing you

down a dirt path
        into a secret hideout of longings
your heart has not forgotten.

And the Fires Will Burn

MICHAEL K. GAUSE

THE LINE WOUND THROUGH the trees like a fuse, and if I craned my neck, I could see where we were headed. As each coat and scarf faded past the entrance, the glow seemed to get brighter. Even now the spirits were visible in random, bobbing procession against the tree line. It was unsettling, all these people, me in the middle, all waiting at dusk. It was good, though. It was good I was here. After all that had happened. It needed to be opened. It would be better after that.

It was another Halloween and, true to the season, the haunting BareBones Halloween performance was about to begin. Set at the Hidden Falls north entrance, this place already ripe with magic for me. (I saw a fairy in the water there back in '95 when I moved here. No lie. But that's another story.) The faces of spirits glow above and around you in dark, positive magic. Shadows made flesh skitter from the dark. Fires flash, then sleep. Binding it all, a live soundtrack performed just out of sight by jerking silhouettes in love with sound.

As I rounded the last curve in the queue, it was starting—stick spiders three people tall, faceless faces floating in the light of smoke. I felt a hand on my shoulder, and I entered.

I had been here before, two years ago now. That year my brother and I laid our father to rest after a long battle with life's hardest hits. How he held on as long as he did is the only mystery about his death. There was love and hate and fear and, later, hope.

So two years later, and here I was again, in both ways. They say losing a father is hard, but that no loss compares to that of a mother, crone, nurturer, the one who brings you into this world. The theme this year seemed spot on, "And the Fires Will Burn." Change, the cycles of loss and hope, the resilience we become to keep it all moving.

I took the Haunted Path down the site, stopping once to watch glowing pods wrestle with the dying and the birth of what comes next. I saw my mother, swaddled like an infant. She was always cold toward the end, her cocoon a sky blue of one hundred percent cotton. I took a seat on the cold ground in what felt like a primal congregation. I'll admit I almost didn't want it to start because that would make it real.

Soon the Fates took stage, weaving their everything webs, the victories and losses of each of us here flowing along, not one thing more important than another. My father was in there making his rounds. And this year my mother would take her place in that infinite procession. Performers arrived and left like breath, plant life and raging water showing us the power of resilience. After a lesson on the baggage we burden ourselves down with, it was all burned clean in a spectacular dirge and dance making way for new growth.

My mother died February 24 in a room where I slept, and I realized I was here to use the thin veil between worlds to share some space, one last time. It was the Calling of the Names, where each and all are invited to speak a name of one now passed. No more waiting. I called her name strong and loud toward the stars, into the twirling fires of dancing wraiths:

Annie June Gause

And as the sound joined others in the webs of past and future, I felt a pain and then peace. I watched as she and the others rose, evaporated into the late October sky, taking their proper place in the world inside us.

Future Hunger

BY AAROHI NARAIN

Burnished sausage
Sticky purple rice
Styrofoam box
of untold joy

You leave Saint Paul
For good
With kua txob kisses
On your lips

at the end of my street the tower still stands

MARSHA FOSS

piece by piece the body of the building falls
crumbling, like a body in hospice fails

after all prayers for survival, that all will be well
after all valiant efforts have failed
begins violent destruction

the tower still stands

removal of the cross
excruciating,
not without cries

the tower still stands

disfigurement and scarring
monotonous sounds of collapse
grinding away dusty debris
of brick and tile, glass and plaster,
pipes and organ gone

under moonlit sky the tower still stands

pain grows each day, day by day
neighbors and friends
bid farewell
during this long vigil
not faring well

the tower still stands

soon with a final swing of the crane
and a crashing rattle she will be gone
negative space where once beauty stood
the soul of a neighborhood diminished

yet in my mind
she will stand at the end of my street
in my heart

At the ruin of St. Andrew's Catholic Church,
Como Park, Saint Paul, Minnesota
August 2019

July 7, 1992

ANNE DIMOCK

It was a hot, late afternoon and the air was buzzing when I went outside. There had been a terrible accident but I did not know that yet. I had worked a little later than usual and was about to go home. I worked at the main hospital downtown—the old "Ancker," the "County," "Ramsey" at the time of this story, now "Regions"— the Level One Trauma Center for the east metro area.

The cold conditioned air escaped a little as the sliding doors passed me through. The dry heat hit me once outside, but something else hit me too. Call it a sixth sense. I knew something had happened, something terrible. But unlike other horrible things that happen in the city that bring broken people to our doorstep, this tragedy lay outside the hospital boundaries.

What I remember most was how there was no way to know. No ambulances in our bay, no police cars, no "code blue" announcements—nothing in the hospital. And there wouldn't be. The bodies would go directly to the morgue. As soon as the sliding doors closed behind me, the fine hairs on my face prickled with static, and I looked to the sky. Clear. Blue. But unsettled. My eyes darted around trying to register what was wrong, what was out of place, which of these things was not like the others. It was a few seconds before I heard the *thwop, thwop, thwop* of helicopters, but they were not ours, they were from the TV stations.

I walked to my car taking in the scene around me—no traffic, no emergency vehicles, no sirens. But there were more people standing outside. Were they drawn to the galvanic air as I was, wondering what was wrong, trying to figure it out? Was there a dignitary in town or a criminal car chase? No, there was just the charged atmosphere and the saliva gathering in my mouth.

I'm not a seer, I have no special powers, but I have a connection to death. Sometimes I know when someone close to me has died or is about to. Like when Susan called to me from deep within her dying, and asleep I answered, "Take whatever you need of me to get through this." She did. And when I stopped everything to sit down and wait for the next phone call, knowing it would be from my mother telling me her brother had died. It was.

I got into my car in the Ramsey Hospital parking lot with the certain knowledge that death was visiting close by. Funny that I never feel that inside the hospital. I pulled out onto Jackson Street and entered the ramp to I-94, still looking for what was amiss. 6 p.m. and hot. Had I left an hour earlier when I usually do, I might have actually seen it happen.

Just on the other side of the river, between Holman Field and the frontage road, two twin-engine planes had collided in midair, raining their wreckage and passengers onto a field. Two people in each plane—nobody knew their names yet. One plane was landing, the other taking off, and they met each other in the restive summer air.

Did they see each other before impact, or were they in each other's blind spots? One practicing their takeoffs and landings, the other coming home, then they're tumbling from the sky. They landed upside down, a short way off the interstate, just to the right of where I was driving. But I didn't know yet, and I couldn't see anything because of the embankment. There was no fire or smoke, just tendrils of febrile energy in the Saint Paul air, and me catching a whiff of it as I went by. "Take whatever you need from me," I whispered, and drove east until home.

A Saint Paul Love Story

ANNA MARIE ETTEL

W. B. YEATS WRITES of "being rooted in one dear perpetual place."
For Jim Mann and me, that was Saint Paul.

When we met in 1971, I was a teacher at Marshall Junior High
School, he was a Saint Paul cop with a police community assign-
ment that took him into neighborhood schools. I was twenty-four,
he was forty-eight. I was white, he was Black. We were an improb-
able couple.

The first time we met, he told me all about myself—where I
lived, the car I drove, where I shopped. Today we'd call it "stalking,"
though we didn't know the term then. He courted me with John
Donne's love poems, amazed me by knowing about "Piers Plow-
man." And he wrote me love poems—I was his "Queen of queens,
ring for my finger, heart of my soul, dream of my dreams." He had
my heart then and kept it for forty years.

Six years of teaching thirteen-year-olds made me realize that I
didn't want to spend the rest of my life doing that. So I went to law
school and worked as a corporate attorney for Minnesota Life for
thirty-two years. He retired as a cop in 1977 and opened a barbecue
restaurant, the Hickory Stick on Selby Avenue. He was a fabulous
cook, but a terrible businessman. After several years, he lost every-
thing—his restaurant, his house, most of his pension. He moved back
to Tennessee, with his five horses, to live with his mother. After four
years apart from me, he was dwindling. I said he should move back to
Saint Paul; somehow we'd make it work. Within a few days, his car
was packed (the horses stayed in Tennessee) and he was on his way.

He worked security at the airport. He went to TVI (now Saint
Paul College), where he got a welding certificate and built a trailer
for his barbecue business. All during the '90s, he sold BBQ at the
Saint Paul Farmers' Market on Saturdays and Sundays and catered
parties. We lived together on the West Side. Our house provided

breathtaking views of downtown Saint Paul, and every Fourth of July family, friends, and neighbors would enjoy the fireworks from our backyard.

He grew old; I guess I did too. In 2007 I couldn't take care of him the way he deserved, so I retired. We went to Cuba, Europe, often to New Orleans for Jazz Fest. We had parties; we filled our life with family and friends, love and laughter.

One day late in 2010, he enrolled in a hospice program. That evening, he asked me to marry him. In all our forty years together, we'd never talked about marriage. But since he wanted to, I said yes. I thought we could have a wonderful party.

On Martin Luther King Jr. Day in 2011 we married, a small ceremony in our home with a Catholic priest for me, an Episcopal deacon for him. I was astounded at how much I delighted in being married to Jim. We planned a party at the Science Museum in April for 200 friends and family. We always did everything backwards.

By July 2011, he was failing, ready to die. I asked him to live until the next Friday so that we could be married for six months. Then I revised my request and asked him to live until I'd finished my wedding thank-you notes. He lived through Friday.

On Saturday morning, one of his oldest friends came to visit. While she was here, I finished writing my thank-you notes. I escorted her to the door, went back to check on him. He'd died. It was one of the few times in his life when he did what I'd asked.

I was bereft. Months after he died, I discovered a poem he'd written to me years before:

> I will be the light
> That twinkles on your windowpane;
> That brightens your path,
> In the dark and the rain,
> And the lonely times.
> Have no fear, I will always be near.

He's been a man of his word.

Last Rites

VALERIE LITTLE

Timor mortis conturbat me
But, we'll be forever this age
thirty-seven and forty-two
now that we've had the last
smile   word
      laugh   embrace
          kiss   ravish
             midnight   morning

I still synthesize you
into my Midwestern cityscape supplications
headphones on before dawn
block early morning noise on the Green Line
draw attention inward
for eye has not seen
ear has not heard
save my eyes so I can recognize you are looking for me
save my ears so I can hear my name in your heart
some city   some street   some day

Honey lips part without sin, act as final anointing
saving us and our body breaks
as wheat and wine for another book of life endured
apart, like before, like next lifetime.
Yet on the floor of my room
I paper over those who caution me
and whisper my intercessions—
as it was in the beginning
is not now and never shall be—
I want you   midnight   morning

on Cathedral Hill's sunlit grass
like the top of Mount Rainier
or the coastal forests of Canada.
You are the unfathomable burn of exploding stars
Callisto   Enceladus   Titania   Triton   Charon
Quiet cadence of urban darkness.
Liminal visions of the sea floor.
Lux aeterna luceat nobis.

Line 1: Fear of death disturbs me.
Line 36: Eternal light, shine on us.

CHAPTER 7
LOVING OUR NEIGHBORS

"It is truly a Hmong renaissance happening to our people in America. We have an explosion not only in arts, but also politics, and commerce, so I encourage all Hmong writers to get their work out to the community. Every voice makes a difference."
—*Ka Vang, Hmong fiction writer, poet, and playwright*

"The arts are an effective bridge for communities who are just starting to learn English to find ways to tell their stories and experiences."
—*Bryan Thao Worra, Hmong writer and poet*

"Life was bitter and I was not. All around me was poverty and sordidness, but I refused to see it that way. By turning it into jokes, I made it bearable."
—*Max Shulman, comedy writer and television producer from Saint Paul*

Winner of 2021
Sidewalk Poetry Contest

Untitled

FILSAN IBRAHIM

Haddii dadku isu yimaadaan oo
midoobaan waxay hanan karaan oo
hagaajin karaan cir dillaacay

Translation from Somali

If people come together
they can even mend
a crack in the sky.

❧ Winner of 2021
Sidewalk Poetry Contest

Untitled

DAWN WING

breathe in
I'm here

breathe out
I belong

Miss Hallie Q. Brown, 1959

CLARENCE WHITE

Clarksdale, Mississippi
is a long way away, longer than
fifty-one years since that long drive
Don't make me do the math

It was more than gas that willed
whatever we drove, dusty noise contraption
that stopping for a drink of the Big Muddy
and wherever that little green book mama
said we could satisfy thirst of car and body

We inched along the route
lined with onlookers, trees
left by men Mr. Roosevelt called to erect
not waving in that still summer
We inch along, slowly; I stick my head
out the window, coaxing some kind of wind

I do not know, this is practice
maybe pre-remembering a day
This is me, Miss Hallie Q. Brown 1959
inching along, slowly, waving in a new summer
princess coaxing a new breeze from still air
top down on this 1959 Bonneville

Today this queen sends many waves
across the avenue, smiles and judgments
my heirs in exile of this kingdom come back
Let me ride the parade, that little crown on my head
and you will know the story, that you come from royals.

Rescue Dog

BETSY LEACH

I AM WALKING THE DOG. Afternoon. Summer. School is out for the year. The neighborhood is more alive with people out, doing things, making noise.

As we walk northward and start down the gentle hill, a young boy is riding his scooter southward, up the hill toward us. At about twenty feet from us, he calls out, cheerfully, that lesson we were never taught as children, "Can I pet your dog?"

"Oh, she would love that," I reply, and already the dog is sitting, ears up, tail sweeping the sidewalk clean behind her, anticipating.

We wait, and the boy approaches. He is maybe seven years old, biracial, skin the color of café au lait, his hair light, dusty brown, and curly. His eyes are green and his gap-toothed smile radiant.

By now, the dog is lying down, sphinx-like, barely able to contain her joy at the thought of childish attention.

He drops his scooter to the sidewalk and, leaning forward, comes down to her level before I can even tell him that, to do so, will keep her from jumping all over him. She rolls onto her back, tilts her head to him and he immediately begins the caressing that her posture invites.

The whole process makes me smile.

"She really likes you," I say.

He is intent on sharing this pleasure with her.

"What's her name?" he asks. I answer.

"Is she a poodle?" he asks.

"Part poodle," I say, thinking how knowledgeable he is.

"Is she a rescue dog?" he asks and looks at me directly, his hands continuing their appreciated caress and his green eyes sparkling.

I laugh slightly—more a vocal smile—and reply, "No. We've had her since she was a puppy." I have decided immediately that explaining about dog breeders, that she was my sixtieth birthday present, that I had to wait for her to be born and that she was chosen just for me because I wanted to make sure, for my grandchildren and my cats, that her response to other creatures would be just what I am watching now—that all this information is probably more of an explanation than this young soul needs right now.

He pets her while she licks his face and ears.

And then he looks at me with that trusting intensity that children show when they really want to know, and fully expect, the truth.

"What is a rescue dog?" he asks with a green-eyed laser focus on my face.

"Ah," I say, "sometimes dogs are living in places where they are not well taken care of. They are hurt or don't get what they need. These dogs get rescued and then are put in homes where they will be loved and looked after."

"Oh," he says and breaks his gaze, looks at the dog, never having broken his hand- and heart-felt attention to her. "I thought they were dogs who saved people."

"Well, that's a different kind of rescue dog," I answer, "and she did save me."

The gaze is back to my face. "How did she do that?" and I know I am not going to get away with the previous simple reply and no explanation.

"Lots of ways and every day," I say. "She makes me take her for walks and that keeps me healthy. She shows me every day she loves me. She makes me happy. Those are some of the ways."

"Oh," he acknowledges, then directs all his attention to her once again.

And watching, smiling, happy to my core, I realize, once again, that there are many ways we can be saved.

Posted on the Neighborhood LISTSERV

ALICE OWEN DUGGAN

Giving away pavers from streetcar days. Spring loaded
attic stairs, aluminum pipe, some elbows. Bicycle
found in the park. If you need a chimney cap,

galvanized steel, email me. Squirrels in the attic.
Four 4x4s seven feet long out on the boulevard.
Found on the sidewalk,

stuffed giraffe. Lifetime of the *National Geographic*.
Useless keys. Can someone recommend someone.
My roof, my furnace, my snow, my trees.

Table and chairs, some scratches. If you count by ones
do you get the same total as if you count by twos?
The table and chairs are gone, is this a sonnet?

Anyone know a good handyman? Rainbird sprinklers,
Rubbermaid cooler, small squirrel holes in the top,
covered with duct tape. Does anyone know anyone.

Extra sod. Leftover gravel. Cat got out.

A Rich Man Indeed

TARA FLAHERTY GUY

RECENTLY AN ERRAND TOOK ME over the river on the Marshall Avenue bridge, where I passed one of Saint Paul's most venerable landmarks, Town & Country Club. As I drove past the historic property overlooking the Mississippi River, the years reeled backward and I was suddenly back in the club's dining room, on a wintry Christmas afternoon in the 1980s. I was preparing to marry into a large Irish family—highly successful travel business people in Saint Paul—who had belonged to the Club for years. My prospective parents-in-law traditionally hosted their large family gatherings there on the big holidays. Warm and generous people, they had included my own parents in their Christmas invitation, to the trepidation of my folks, who were not exactly members of Saint Paul's country club set. Both were educated professionals—a registered nurse and a teacher—but the air of Town & Country Club was rather more rarefied than their own atmosphere.

My mother had been born to a hardworking farm family in Redwood Falls that beggared themselves to send her to St. Catherine's for a nursing degree. My dad was born on Dayton's Bluff in Saint Paul, to a hard-drinking blue-collar neighborhood populated mostly with Irish immigrant railroad families like his own, barely upslope from Swede Hollow. Deserted early by his father, Dad was taken from his impoverished mother and put into the care of a series of strangers for what turned out to be all of his formative years. Depression-era foster parents were poor, simply desperate for the scanty income provided by the county; consequently, many foster children went uncared for, or at least unsupervised. Kids like my dad bounced from foster home to foster home, living like street urchins in various Catholic parishes all over Saint Paul, wherever they were deposited next, to register for grade school: St. Mark's, St. Luke's, St. Columba, Holy Childhood, Assumption. Theirs were tough childhoods. Both being highly practical children of the Depression, my parents eschewed anything "fancy schmancy," and anticipated the gathering at the venerated country club dubiously—especially my father.

On Christmas Day the club's dining room was decorated with twinkling Christmas trees, beribboned wreaths, and fragrant pine boughs. Candles glowed, crystal and silver sparkled, and a roaring blaze in the fireplace, flanked by the gracefully arched tall windows overlooking the river, radiated warmth and welcome. Escorted to the boisterous family table in front of windows, we were welcomed warmly to the table and into our soon-to-be expanded family. In no time, conversation began to flow, unease disappeared, and laughter rang out as my dad's worries about differing social strata melted away like butter on warm Irish soda bread. As the afternoon wound down, I glanced at my dad next to me, prepared to tease him about having fretted about "fitting in" with high society. Lost in thought, he was watching the fading sunset over the river. Then I saw the gleam of unshed tears in his eyes. Dismayed, I took his hand. "What is it, Dad?"

"Nothing, sweetie . . . I was just remembering a dirty little boy in a grimy gang of kids playing along that riverbank down there, about a thousand years ago."

"Was the little boy anybody I might know?" I asked gently. He nodded. "We climbed the rocks, all the way up from the river. We pressed our faces up against these very windows, trying to catch a glimpse of the 'rich people' inside." My own eyes misted then, imagining the ragged little boy who would someday be my dad. I leaned over and kissed his cheek. "And here you are . . . one of them," I said, as we rose to leave. He was still contemplative as we collected our coats, and smiled at me, a bit shamefacedly. "I can't believe I had to be reminded today what that lonely little kid didn't know. Genuine wealth isn't found in a bank . . . the real treasure is the love of family and friends." As we went out into the cold Christmas moonlight, my dad took my mom's arm and my own, leaning close to whisper to me, "I am a rich man indeed."

The Woodcarver on West Seventh Street

RAYMOND LUCZAK

As he slowly guides the chunk of linden
wood inside the lathe of his hands
with slashes of knife,
a misshapen orb slowly becoming
the body of a sparrow puffed up
against the winter to come,
all idle thoughts go:
his boy's face.
That beak needs to be smoothed out.
There. Another marriage gone south. Hmm.
That wing is too thick. Just a tiny whit.
Guess it's just me and a little nip.
With his finished bird cradled in hand,
he stands for a moment on the sidewalk,
surrounded by chips curling up
for affection around his feet.

74

LILIA LOBOUGH

METRO TRANSIT BUSES serve a quarter of a million riders each day. I recalled this as I stood with my legs buried to the knee in a snowbank, waiting for the route that could take me home. I pondered why thousands of us chose to stand and wait for these buses, day in and day out, when they wouldn't do us the simple courtesy of arriving on time.

After ten minutes, I had some doubts about continuing my professional relationship with the 74 bus. After all, a business connection should have benefits for both parties. Where was the benefit for me, left stranded in a blizzard with frozen, nonfunctional toes?

When the 74 finally arrived, I fought my way up the snowbank and attempted to get through the doors in an upright position. That didn't happen. I fell into the bus and landed on my knees into the damp, lukewarm air. From my position on the salt-gritted floor I raised my Go Card to tap it to the sensor.

"Sorry for the wait," said the driver, bundled in a coat warmer than my own. If I had to guess, I'd say his toes were not frozen.

"Oh, no worries," I said, "you're fine." And he was! How could I be upset with the man when he'd driven this huge, mobile furnace right up to the spot where I was buried? Being outside in these conditions parallels venturing out into space; at the end of the day, you're just grateful you made it back home.

I got myself semi-upright again and tumbled into the nearest seat, no dignity regained. I didn't care about my knees being wet because everyone else on the 74 was wet too. We smelled like a flock of sheep that had gone swimming. But, as in other seasons, the other riders shut out the external unpleasantness with phones and earbuds. That was alright by me.

With my music turned up, I could retreat into myself with temporary reprieve from the elements. I stared out the foggy window,

challenging myself to assign familiarity to nebulous shapes of build-
ings. Every landmark was obscured by driving snow and a level of
darkness unwelcome at four thirty in the afternoon. The only guide
was the courteous, bored robot voice announcing, "Approaching
Chatsworth Street. Milton Street. Victoria Street."

If not for that voice, we could have been driving in Chicago, in
Reykjavik, or at the North Pole, and been none the wiser. But when
on the 74, I know I'm in Saint Paul because of those around me. This
knowledge had less to do with the number of layers the riders are
sporting, and more to do with the expressions they wear. A winter
bus rider is marked by steeled eyes and a perpetually clenched jaw.
During a commute, they have no patience for small talk or a slow,
hesitant walker. It's more than a matter of survival—it's an adven-
ture in spite. Each successful bus journey is a win against the muf-
fling march of snow and ice.

When my stop approached, I was determined not to face-plant
into the snow. I knew I was close by the warm orbs of streetlights
and stood before we halted at the slush-piled stop. It's impolite to
keep everyone waiting, but I carved out one second to thank the
driver before the doors opened, and I stepped out into space. Stand-
ing on the corner waiting to cross, I watched the glowing number
74 on the rear of the bus fade into the lavender wash of nighttime
snow. I was alone, thoughts and footsteps quieted once more. There
was no guarantee that the bus, or I, would arrive at that spot again
tomorrow.

Winner of 2021
Sidewalk Poetry Contest

Untitled

KYRA ZIMMERMAN

I need people
who will see my cracked self
and not try to play the hero
nor come swooping in
on the wings of "here, cheer up"
nor the mighty flexing arms of advice,
but will sit next to me
and wait for me
to sort out the pieces
while I glue myself together.

To the Man Who Tried to Make Me Smile

BERGEN CHRISTOFFER EIBS

To the man who tried to make me smile,

I want to tell you that I'm sorry for pushing you away.

I remember seeing you on the corner of Pascal Street and St. Anthony Avenue near Allianz Field in Saint Paul. I remember your purple sweatshirt, your ginger hair and beard, your toothy grin.

You saw the tears streaming down my face while I sat in my car waiting for the light to change. I was desperate to get back onto Highway 94, only to see it closed for roadwork. I was having a hectic day. I had just worked at a deli eight hours straight, where rude customers yelled at me for not understanding their vague orders. I had a lot of difficult online math homework I had barely gotten done; I was scared I was going to fail because my grades on the assignments didn't look so hot. I had a fight with my family. We were all stressed about getting stuff done around the house, while I wondered when I could go back to my dorm at St. Catherine University to get away from the fighting.

When I saw you taking a few steps to my car, I got scared because I thought you might have bad intentions. I thought you wanted to break my window and rob or assault me. I was so vulnerable I couldn't think straight. When I was inching my car up while desperately waiting for the light to turn green, I wasn't trying to run you over. I was keeping my guard up.

It wasn't until I saw you point at your big grin after the light turned green that I wondered, what *were* your true intentions? You didn't want to hurt me. You wanted to help me. I felt the regret of pushing you away sink in. I think back to those brief seconds when I recognized that I don't have to be alone when I'm at my worst. You helped me look forward to the future and forget the bad day I had. It made me feel grateful that a stranger wanted to look out for me. That is the true meaning of the kind Saint Paul spirit.

If you're out there somewhere in Saint Paul or elsewhere, I want to let you know that I'm smiling now.

Recipe for a Laurel Avenue Meringue

SARA DOVRE WUDALI

Take one unused trampoline from your backyard.
Give it to the family three doors down who most ask to jump.

Remark on the trampoline-sized hole in your dandelion plain.
Stir the dirt, plant clover, and embrace lawn flowers.

Notice the crabapple, whose leaves shiver
every time you light the fire pit.

Move the pit to the center of the crop circle
so sparks can jump under open sky.

Watch the wasps kiss the clothespins in the sun.
Someone should notice their unrequited affection.

Pull out the old vertical privacy fence.
Together, build a new one with horizontal slats,

tighten the boards to keep puppies safe,
but leave sufficient space for community.

Add gates but forget to shut them.
Treat the neighbor's dog when he comes to visit.

Pass each other sugar and eggs, stir with a stalk of rhubarb.

◦ჳ Winner of 2021
Sidewalk Poetry Contest

Untitled

DIANA LEASKAS

Sending warmth if you are cold
Forgiveness if you are blamed
Justice if you are persecuted
Love around the globe

CHAPTER 8

HONORING MOTHER EARTH

"Is there not something worthy of perpetuation in our Indian spirit democracy, where Earth, our mother, was free to all, and no one sought to impoverish or enslave his neighbor."
—*Ohiyesa (Charles Eastman), Dakota author*

"We used to content ourselves by thinking we knew all about our world, at least; but now it is different, and we wonder if we really know anything, or if there can be safety and peace anywhere in the wide universe."
—*Donald Wandrei, science fiction writer*

"All that was good will never be gone. . . . All that was good is seen today and tomorrow in the strivings of those we know, towards dignity, compassion, and respect for their fellow man and his community."
—*William Hoffman, Jewish writer*

Breathe

JIM BOUR

Early morning chill
Spring, singing, dandelions
a bird in the bath

Summer egg grows legs
dill and milkweed wave goodbye
monarch butterfly

Cold hard frozen lawn
full throttle dandelions
under the white sheet

Two Guerrillas Doing Good

HEIDI SCHALLBERG

I WAS TIRED OF LOOKING AT the neglected enormous concrete planters dumped in the circle drive behind my bus stop. They hunkered there in two groups of four against a backdrop of black plastic shrouding the old Ford plant site. The circle drive had been an old streetcar turnaround in the day; now it was mostly used by utility trucks and Metro Transit maintenance vehicles.

My mom had died earlier that year, and I still wasn't functioning well from grief. Why not, I thought, try a little guerrilla gardening? In grief, I wanted to grow and create. I needed to do things with my hands because my brain wasn't working, and those neglected planters begged for my attention.

I found myself at Menards, buying a big bag of dirt. Although I wanted to clear out all four of the planters closest to the bus stop, I knew I should start with just one at first. They were big. Besides, a duck had been using the last one as a nest.

I cleared out inches of the old soil and covered it with fresh dirt. A coworker alerted me to appropriate free plants on a local Facebook gardening group. A woman who lived close by gave me free catmint, along with johnny jump ups. I planted them, spread mulch, watered, and waited. The Menards bucket I hid behind the planter to collect rainwater disappeared, so without a nearby water source, I lugged water from my apartment blocks away or hoped for rain. Some mornings I would get to the bus stop a few minutes early so I could check on my plants. Although the state of the planters indicated my work would likely be left alone, I was aware this unauthorized experiment could end at any time. I bought a rainbow-colored pinwheel and stuck it at the front of the planter as a cheery note. Maybe I could eventually create a mosaic on these dismal bunkers.

Three months into my experiment, I arrived at my bus stop one morning to find all eight planters empty. No more catmint, tall weeds, or the fountain grass someone had planted long ago in one of the others. My bus pulled up, so I had to board.

Shocked, I had to wait until after work to inspect the damage. No more pinwheel, which was gone. Everything was chopped off, pulled out. Who would do that, and why? No one had paid any attention to these for the past couple of years. Why now?

A day or so later, I was walking home and saw our neighborhood volunteer handyman pruning trees in the circle drive. I'd see him everywhere in this area in his yellow safety vest, chipping ice off curb ramps, picking up trash, pruning trees, and clearing old raggedy weeds.

"Hi!" I greeted him. He told me he'd been working long hours here the past couple of days clipping the trees back and the weeds out of the planters. "Yeah, those had looked bad for a long time," I said truthfully. I thanked him for paying attention to this end of the street, which many forget about because of the long vacant land behind it. He said he does what he does for the kids. He wants to set a good example for them and show them they can make their world better.

I never mentioned the gardening I had attempted in one of the planters. My wish had come true. Someone cared enough about this little neglected corner of my neighborhood to make it look better, and it did. Soon after, the planters were moved to another spot, and I no longer had to wait for the bus while scheming to counter their abandonment.

The Day the River Smiled

YARA OMER

I LEFT THE DOCTOR'S OFFICE heading to work. Instead, I drove to the Mississippi.

I work on the West Side but I live twenty minutes away. Each time I take exit 242D, I am greeted by the tall buildings touching the clouds. By the time I make it to Robert Street, I am ready to embrace my crossing of the Mississippi. I think of myself twenty-two years ago, in a far continent, in a city that lacked natural bodies of water. Aside from my dreams, I never thought I would see the big river.

Twice a day, for eleven years now, my heart dances when I cross it. Every time, I contemplate that I never go near the water. Today, I did.

I parked next to the Padelford harbor. I would've loved to walk alongside the river looking at the boats. I could get lost in this amazing scene for hours. I needed to get to work in ten minutes, and my foot was aching, awaiting physical therapy in the hope of averting surgery.

I sat. I was there alone except for another man who walked past me. He had earbuds in and greeted me with a smile.

People's smiles in Minnesota are greatly appreciated, gravely needed, but could be a challenge for me to interpret. Some of them do not reveal much. Per definition, a smile is a gesture that shows friendliness and welcoming. His, though, which only lasted a second or two, left me void. His eyes did not smile. I do not know how, but he froze his face moving only his lips.

Nonetheless, I appreciated it. I took it as an "I mean you no harm; just leave me alone" smile. I returned it the only way I know—using my entire face—and looked back at the river.

I wanted to forget my foot. Effortlessly, my eyes went to the boats, and time stopped. I became part of the harbor. Things were still and so was I. The boats were not moving, aside from the gentle nudges of the waves. I took a few steps toward the rusty fence and did not feel comfortable leaning on it or touching it, so I stood there studying the water.

The Mississippi was dirty. I let out a sigh. I was taught that river water is fresh and drinkable. I had always dreamt of scooping a cold sip with my hands and washing my face in a river. Both the Mississippi and the Nile crushed my expectations with their murky water and strong smells. I breathed out my disappointment and looked up.

I saw the colored buildings, the Cathedral, and the life this river has been nurturing for centuries. It hit me; not a single drop of water I see now will be here again. It will keep flowing, never coming back to this spot. Not a single wave is the same as another, no matter how identical they may seem. I would be a liar to claim that I have seen the Mississippi; no matter how many times I look at it, I will never truly see it.

I stood there with a new sense of hope. A day will come when the Mississippi is crystal clear for me to drink from it, and I will be able to wash my face in the Nile. A day will come when I am able, once again, to walk down the street, ride a horse, or stand and admire the riverbank on Harriet Island, with no pain.

I smiled the kind of smile that moved not only my entire face but also my heart. I looked at the Mississippi River. It smiled back. My ten minutes had passed. I walked slowly to my car.

Six minutes later, I was at work.

Mississippi

THERESA JAROSZ ALBERTI

Since the Pleistocene Age
you have worn a groove
through this land,
patient waters
like a finger rubbing
again and again. Some
have called you Old Man
River, but to me you are
Missus, a wise one,
old and going strong.

You have seen the heart of this country,
kept a steady pulse, from Lake Itasca
to the Gulf of Mexico. You've seen my heart too,
as I walk the River Road, listened as my footsteps pounded
and my head raced ahead stumbling, fretting.
You never laughed, your kind ear leaning
toward me.

I have been afraid all my life. I am afraid
to walk down the path to your woodsy banks
alone. Someone is always coming
after me in dreams. I recheck doors
I know I've locked. I admonish my children
to chew grapes carefully, not play with them
in their mouth. Never play on the railroad tracks.
Never swim in the river.

Your comforting hum makes me forget your pulsing current.
You carry barges, Missus, have worked
tirelessly pushing glacier-melted waters
for two million years. How many humans
have walked beside you, spilling out fears like rose petals?

You are nine feet deep, you are one hundred feet deep.
You are but a stream at your source, you are 4,500 feet wide in
    Illinois.
I don't know what to believe about you when I walk
looking down the bluff at smooth water.
How many bones have you carried? Buried?

I know you won't tell. You are here to listen
after all. Patiently carry the water, push the barges,
witness land and life. It is ever changing, it is
always the same. Your steady heartbeat.
My fears are nothing new.

Please, Missus, catch these petals, carry them.
Flow them past the delta, let them enter
the greater ocean,
the greater mystery.

Sue's Park

ROGER BREZINA

Her house no longer stands
on the corner lot of the little, rural town
that no longer *is* a little, rural town.
Her house left this world
after Sue left this world
and she left this world
her peaceful, corner lot
as a piece of unspoiled ground.
It's Sue's Park now.
No indication of foundation—
not a single brick remains.
The corner lot instills some fame,
keeps her memory through time
where children play and read the sign
that says "Sue's Park"—
a gift of love by death—
a little lot that bears the name
of the all-but-forgotten Sue.
Enter an unknown artist who
had drawn the park on paper
then crumpled their work into a ball
and dropped it on the lawn for all
to find as trash, pick up, discard,
but where it beckoned me
to keep Sue's memory
in case a callous city grew
to make obscurity of Sue.
Her world was squirrels and birds,
chipmunks and rabbits braving near,
and children playing she endeared.

I never knew the absent Sue,
but on a little lot with a lot of love
Sue is remembered here.
Sue's Park is gone now—
swallowed by the city—
and all that remains of her memory
is the crumpled-up drawing
by artist anonymous
that I'd found on the grass
and the sentimental ditty
I'd written on that day.

Spring Garden

SARA MARTIN

THERE WAS A THICK BLANKET OF SNOW on the ground when we packed up the house that was our home for over eighteen years and had our belongings trucked across the river. The blanket had been even thicker when we toured our new home, icicles lining the gutters, two stories plus an attic above. We had no clue what the snow hid around the house or in our small backyard. But as the days grew longer and warmer, the snow melted into rivulets trickling down our driveway and front walk, and I cut away the remains of last year's blooms, tiny green shoots worked their way through partially composted leaves.

My son and I track the progress of the clematis on the south side of the house every afternoon as we return from school, its vines reaching up to the six-foot trellis anchored to the chimney brick, stretching for the next rung each day. Just a month after the first shoots appeared, it has surpassed the trellis, using minute cracks in the stucco as holds to scale the chimney.

Sprigs of catmint are also among the first to surface. As I rub the leaves between my thumb and forefinger to release the sage and mint scent, I am brought back to the spring eighteen years ago when I built my last garden from a blank-palette yard of mostly dirt and scraggly grass, and a haphazard collection of shrubs the previous owners hadn't managed to kill. That yard, unlike this one, had not been well loved or well tended to. We nursed that yard to life with soil amendments, grass seed, and perennials dug up from friends' gardens, transported in buckets, divided, and planted in the dark Minnesota topsoil. That summer, after Dutch elm disease took the towering tree on our boulevard, we planted an amur chokecherry, chosen for its gold bark, which I thought would brighten the winter landscape. And it did, until straight-line winds took it down twelve years later.

I'm most excited to see the globe-shaped peonies growing larger each day. Soon ants will crawl onto the globes, eat the glue, and release the deep pink blooms.

I've refrained from planting much in the new garden, waiting to see what else surfaces throughout the growing season. What I have planted, though, is a raised-bed herb garden on the south side of the house near the clematis trellis. As my son and I tend to it daily, I show him how to rub the leaves between his fingers and to inhale the sweet or spicy scent left behind. I pluck leaves of tarragon or cilantro or basil and give him one, keeping one for myself, so we can taste what will flavor our dinners later this summer.

On the boulevard of our new house is an elm tree, likely a half century old, as it was here when the previous owners bought the home forty years ago from the original owners who built the house in 1925. This morning on our driveway we find an evacuated robin's egg. I cradle the blue shell in my palm. My son inspects where the new robin broke through the surface with its egg tooth to take its first breath of air as its mother sang in their nest high in our tree. The shell, like the plants that stretch toward the sun, is a delicate reminder that in spring all things begin anew.

Living with West End Wildlife

DEANNE L. PARKS

I LIVE IN THE West End of Saint Paul. According to our neighborhood Facebook page, "West Seventh Is Where the Cool Kids Hang Out," so this makes me a "Cool Kid." When Cool Kids aren't arguing over who has the best pizza or commiserating over their disdain for the band Nickelback, they often post about local wildlife. We have raccoons that spy on you from the sewer grates as you walk past, their eyes reflecting red in the dark like little gutter gremlins. There are turkeys that roost on parked cars. Kevin, the ubiquitous albino squirrel, is everyone's favorite. Like Santa, there is only one Kevin. One April Fools' Day, someone posted a Photoshopped image of what appeared to be a dead white squirrel on West Seventh Street. Distraught Cool Kids weighed in on the thread causing the poster to repeatedly explain, "It was just a joke!" But the most talked about wildlife in the West End is without a doubt, the garter snakes.

There is a diagonal line that runs through the neighborhood. On one side, folks who have lived here all their lives have never seen a snake. On the other side, well, we're crawling with them.

They say it has to do with the geology of the area and our close proximity to the Mississippi River. It's been suggested that a West End flag be created with a garter snake on it. A friend in real estate told me potential home buyers will ask on which side of the snake line a property is located.

We installed a small water feature in our backyard and as the saying goes, "Build it and they will come." The snakes are in heaven. They sun themselves on the rocks and hold well-attended spring procreation parties. When they want to cool off, they go for a dip in the cement pond, happily swimming in circles and floating on the lily pads. The snakes are a benefit in that they eat insects and rodents. My husband grew up in Iowa chasing all manner of creatures around rivers and creeks. He loves the snakes. I get that. But I grew up in the South around the venomous variety and so it's taken some getting used to. Whenever I see one, I let out a short, involuntary shriek. Sometimes this is followed by the sound of my neighbors on the other side of the fence laughing.

One hot summer day, my husband and I were walking from the house to the garage when a snake shot across the path in front of me. I shrieked, no surprise there, but then my legs took off running without my permission. Our yard is very small and so to keep from running into the fence, I turned and ran back where I came from, where there is also a fence. I continued to run back and forth, shrieking, with zero control over my legs and going nowhere. My husband, who is old enough to collect Social Security, became a ten-year-old boy. He ran to catch the snake before it could dive into the water feature. Just as he grabbed the snake's tail, he slipped on some loose gravel causing him to throw the snake high into the air. I'm still running back and forth, but now between shrieks I'm screaming at him, *"Ahhh! What are you doing? Ahhh!"*

I looked up to see the snake flying through the air in a graceful, slow-motion dance against blue sky filled with puffy white clouds. It sailed over the fence and into the neighbor's backyard. My feet stopped running. My shrieking stopped. My heart was pounding. My husband and I stared at each other in silence and then started to giggle. That's about the time the neighbors started screaming.

Harbinger from Nature

ANDREA E. JOHNSON

Outside a renovated building in Lowertown Saint Paul,
    two yellow-bellied sapsuckers
lay lifeless on the ground.
    They were perfect in death,

dignified and dapper,
    sporting blackest black and whitest white
checked and striped jackets,
    topped by fiery red crowns upon their heads.

I could see but a trace of yellow
    and wondered if a brush of sap
on their spotted bellies
    might flash a brighter color in flight.

They looked like Fabergé jeweled miniatures
    lying on the sidewalk
opposite the Farmers' Market,
    one on the damp gray concrete

the other on a metal grate
    ringing a bare city tree.
A morning mist magnified their radiance.
    I could see no mar on their bodies.

A stopping passerby speculated
    the birds succumbed to toxins
sprayed on old buildings
    to poison nests of pigeons.

Vivid, yet still, their tiny corpses lay
    at the foot of the historic structure.
They were mates to their last breath,
    victims of something ominous,

a loss, I fear,
    greater than anything gained,
for their sudden demise
    is a grave harbinger among us.

Sacred Water

DIANE WILSON

DURING THE SIXTEEN YEARS I lived in Saint Paul, I grew to love the lone tamarack that lived in the backyard of my little bungalow, far from its natural habitat farther north. This majestic tree turned a dusky gold in autumn before shedding its needles. In spring, it attracted aphids that drew a visit from the ruby-crowned kinglet, a tiny khaki-colored bird that was one of several hundred species that followed the Mississippi River flyway during migration.

As much as I loved Saint Paul, I couldn't resist the opportunity to move an hour north to a place with ten acres that included a tamarack bog. After reading about the bog in the house listing, I drove through an ice storm the next morning to see it. Behind the house stood several acres of tall, skeletal tamaracks bare of needles, branches dusted with snow. The bog was a sanctuary for birds and pitcher plants, surrounded by well-worn deer trails.

In the years since I left Saint Paul to steward this bog, I have learned how dependent this unique habitat is on water. In spring, the snowmelt replenishes the moat that surrounds the bog, spilling over to refresh nearby marshy areas that are home to spring peeper frogs, their song a delightful, cacophonous declaration of the season. The jungle call of the pileated woodpecker is complemented by the rough song of the sandhill crane that nests nearby. Since my house is within a few miles of the St. Croix River, I'm still visited in spring by migrating birds that use the river as a flyway, just as Indigenous people had used the river as a trade route for thousands of years.

As a Dakota woman from the Mdewakanton Oyate, I do my best to uphold the teaching Mitakuye Owasin: We Are All Related. This means I have a responsibility to care for the land and the water that nourishes it. On a practical, daily level, there are things I can do, such as conserve water, express gratitude through prayer, and avoid using pesticides and fertilizers that could be washed downhill by the rain into the bog. But there is another, deeper level of understanding that informs how I care for this place.

The Oceti Sakowin, or Seven Council Fires, which includes the Dakota, Lakota, and Nakota peoples, carries an origin story that teaches the sacred nature of water. This relationship is embedded in our language, our understanding of the world, and our cosmology. The elders teach us that water is every being's first medicine.

At a time when modern-day thinking values water as a resource to be used, negotiated, and sold, we have to remember what it means to be in an Indigenous relationship with this precious relative. The courageous people at the Standing Rock Indian Reservation in North and South Dakota who challenged the Keystone XL pipeline showed us how to protect what we love, to always remember Mni Wiconi, water is life. Not to *protest* the short-term thinking of an extractive industry, but to *protect*—a critical difference in the way we view the world. In the words of Tiokasin Ghosthorse, Cheyenne River, "We are not defending Mother Earth. We are Mother Earth in defense of herself."

Make of yourself a light, Photograph, Bianca Pettis, *Almanac* 2014

Untitled

CHONG YANG

Cia lub ntiaj teb los ua koj lub vaj
Tus njuj neeg yog ib lub paj, xim twg los zoo
Txoj kev tsaus ntuj yuav tsis kav
Ib pliag xwb, cia nws dhau
Es lub paj mam nthuav

Translation from Hmong

Let this world be your garden
Each person a flower, lovely in every hue
Darkness descends, but not for long
It is a season, so let it pass
And the peony opens

CONTRIBUTORS' NOTES

THERESA JAROSZ ALBERTI is a writer, blogger, artist, and creator living in Minneapolis, Minnesota. She writes all kinds of things, including seven books of children's nonfiction and a book of poetry. You can find her online at penandmoon.com.

MARC ANDERSON is a Saint Paul percussionist, poet, composer, Zen priest, grandfather, teacher, part-time nomad, full-time enthusiast.

LEILANI ANDREWS is a young woman who loves to learn and experiment with life. When she's not working or in school, she enjoys arts such as writing, painting, photography, acting, and studying film. She doesn't know what she wants to do with her life but is excited for what the future may bring.

PAUL BARD is a fourth-generation Saint Paulite. He has only ever lived in two ZIP codes, and they are contiguous.

HEIDI BARR is committed to cultivating ways of being that are life-giving and sustainable for people, communities, and the planet. Co-founder of 12 Tiny Things (12TinyThings.com), she works as a wellness coach, holds a master's degree in faith and health ministries, and partners with organic farms and yoga teachers to offer retreat experiences. She lives with her husband and daughter and they tend a large vegetable garden, explore nature, and do their best to live simply. Visit her at heidibarr.com.

HANNAH BOEHME is a queer illustrator and writer, born and raised in Saint Paul. She is an MCAD alum whose previous work includes portraiture for the Ramsey County Historical Society. Her art specializes in bright, colorful scenes and warm moments shared between characters. More of her work can be found @hboehme01 on Instagram or at hannahboehme.com.

JIM BOUR lives and plays out his good fortune in Saint Paul, Minnesota. He loves to write and tell stories, walk and cycle the neighborhoods, and work to make where he lives a safe, inviting, and just place.

AMANDA BOYLE is a first-generation student and currently has an Undecided major. Writing has always been an outlet for her life. With immigrant family members and parents, she has plenty of stories with a foundation of culture.

ROGER BREZINA has written over 9,900 poems. Some are factual, some fictitious, some historical, some hysterical. Raised on a farm in south-central Minnesota, he graduated from college after complicating his mind. He now resides on five acres of the old homestead trying to uncomplicate his mind.

WENDY BROWN-BAEZ is the author of *Heart on the Page: A Portable Writing Workshop*. Her poetry and prose appear widely in literary journals and anthologies, such as *Mizna, Poets & Writers, Talking Writing, Water~Stone Review*, and *Tiferet*. Wendy facilitates writing workshops in community spaces and has been lucky enough to be part of Saint Paul Almanac for years. You can find more about her online at wendybrownbaez.com.

COLLEEN CASEY lives in a tiny sky-blue bungalow near Como Lake. She has turned her little yard into a paradise for birds, bees, butterflies, and other pollinators by planting it full of native wildflowers that bloom spring through fall. Of mixed Dakota and Euro-American heritages, she sees herself as a person of crosscurrents and confluences and believes we are all related.

TY CHAPMAN is a Twin Cities–based puppeteer, poet, curator, and storyteller. His upcoming works include writing a children's book through the Loft's Mirrors and Windows program and creating a one-man shadow puppet and marionette show for Puppet Lab.

LEQUETTA DIGGS is a resident of Falcon Heights, Minnesota, who enjoys reading, painting with watercolors, promoting childhood and adult literacy, and campaigning for equity and social justice. She is an active member of the Baha'i Faith and The Cultural Wellness Center's Elder Coaching Program, as well as the proud mother of twins, Martin and Michael, and four beautiful, gifted grandchildren.

ANNE DIMOCK is a narrative writer working in fiction and creative nonfiction. Her memoir, *Humble Pie—Musings on What Lies Beneath the Crust*, was a finalist for a Minnesota Book Award. She has received awards, fellowships, and residencies for her narrative writing and has been published in print and online journals. Her new book, *Against the Grain*, will be published in November 2022 by Woodhall Press.

LOUIS DISANTO worked as a keeper at Saint Paul's Como Zoo for over twenty years before retiring in 2005. He was also a photographer/reporter for the weekly *Saint Paul Sun* and an information specialist for the City of Saint Paul. His interests include classical music, sports, writing children's stories, and getting together with friends. Louis is honored to be one of the winners of the 2011 Saint Paul Sidewalk Poetry Contest.

NORITA DITTBERNER-JAX has published five collections of poetry, most recently *Crossing the Waters* (Nodin Press, 2017), winner of the Midwest Book Award in Poetry, and *Now I Live Among Old Trees* (Nodin Press, 2020). Norita has won other awards for her work, including several nominations for the Pushcart Prize. A poetry editor for Red Bird Chapbooks, she lives in Saint Paul, Minnesota.

ARIA DOMINGUEZ was born and grew up in Saint Paul and now lives in Minneapolis with her son. Though she has not lived in Saint Paul for a long time, it is the thread forming the fabric of so many memories, and the foundation of who she became.

SARA DOVRE WUDALI is a writer and editor from Saint Paul, Minnesota. Her work has been published or is forthcoming in *Creative Nonfiction, Sweet, North Dakota Quarterly,* and *Saint Paul Almanac,* and has appeared as part of a public art project in Mankato, Minnesota.

Poems by ALICE OWEN DUGGAN have appeared in *Tar River Poetry, Alaska Quarterly Review, Poetry East,* and elsewhere, as well as in a chapbook, *A Brittle Thing,* and an anthology, *Home,* from Holy Cow! Press. She's interested in dailiness, in plain speech, in the timbre of voices in telling stories.

BERGEN CHRISTOFFER EIBS is a writer who received a bachelor's degree in English from St. Catherine University in May 2021. She hopes to publish her own novels and other short stories in the future. When she's not working on her writing, she is collecting enamel pins or spending time with her fiancé.

Born in Saint Paul in 1946, ANNA MARIE ETTEL lived almost all her life within five miles of downtown Saint Paul. She is a retired corporate attorney, but now calls herself a community builder. She says that's a lot more fun.

MARSHA FOSS enjoys Saint Paul's vibrant writing community. A retired educator, she divides her time between Minnesota and Maryland. When in her Como Park neighborhood, she has the fun of living near young grandsons. Her work has been published online and in print journals, and she has been nominated for a Pushcart Prize.

ANNETTE GAGLIARDI has published poetry in *Jitter Press, Poetry Quarterly, Dreamers Creative Writing* and their year one anthology,

Down in the Dirt Magazine, and *Poetic Bond VIII* and *IX.* Annette is a contributor and co-editor of *Upon Waking: 58 Voices Speaking Out from the Shadow of Abuse.* She teaches poetry at a nearby elementary school as a volunteer. She has won two national and six state awards for her poetry.

MICHAEL K. GAUSE was born in Tennessee while The Beatles were still together. He visited Minnesota in 1995 and never went back. His writing can be found in print and online. His piece "The Sentinel" was published in Volume 2 of *Saint Paul Almanac.*

CASEY GORDON has been in the Twin Cities for three years and is in her first year with Saint Paul Almanac. She has taught literature, writing, and changemaking at the City University of New York and the University of St. Thomas. She loves music and "Minnesota Experience" on TPT and has finally learned how to dress for the weather.

CATHERINE BOEBEL GROTENHUIS and her husband, Steve, raised their blended family in Saint Paul and help with their local grandchildren. She worked at Women's Advocates, the Farmington Senior Center, and the Science Museum of Minnesota's Youth Science Center. Raised on Chicago's South Side, she graduated from Carleton College and has been published in several online publications. Her nonfiction manuscript is seeking publication.

ISADORA GRUYE is a writer and photographer living in Minnesota. She believes in cartographers and beekeepers but has little need for maps or honey. She is the editor and co-founder of *Nice Cage* literary magazine, and her work has appeared in many places in the tactile and virtual world. Her poetry collection *The Ladies' Guide to the Apocalypse* was published in October 2019.

TARA FLAHERTY GUY is a contributing writer at Saint Paul Publishing Company, and a graduate of the creative writing program at

Metropolitan State University in Saint Paul, Minnesota. Born and raised in Saint Paul, she is a devotee of both the Saintly City and the beloved *Almanac* named for it.

CARLA HAGEN lives, writes, and bicycles in Saint Paul, where she is revising her second novel. She loves open-water swimming, good coffee, and languages of all kinds.

MARGARET HASSE is a poet, teacher, and editor of other poets' work. Her fifth book of poetry, *Between Us*, won the poetry prize of the Midwest Independent Publishers Association.

JUDY HAWKINSON lives in Saint Paul, where she and her husband raised their three children. She enjoys writing, photography, hiking, and spending time with her family and friends.

LISA HIGGS's third chapbook, *Earthen Bound*, was published by Red Bird Chapbooks in February 2019. Her poems have been published widely, and her reviews and interviews can be found at *Poetry Foundation, Kenyon Review*, and *The Adroit Journal*.

JORDAN HIRSCH wishes she could spend all of her time watching *Star Trek*, but she also enjoys cooking, reading, writing, and running, so she spends time doing that too. Originally from southern Illinois, she lives in the Como Park neighborhood with her husband and their two perfect cats.

TERRANCE HOBSON II is a self-deprecating Minnesotan with ties to Mississippi. He is an aspiring music producer who attended the High School for Recording Arts in Saint Paul. New to poetry, he draws on personal experience and finds relief in writing what he doesn't talk about.

ALIA JERAJ is a vocalist, writer, and educator in the Twin Cities. She has performed with groups including Mixed Precipitation, Artemis, and Nanilo. Her bylines include *POLLEN, Twin Cities Daily Planet,* and *American Craft*. By day she tutors math at a local high school.

ANDREA E. JOHNSON grew up in West Saint Paul. She earned bachelors degrees in piano and nursing at the University of Minnesota and an M.Ed. degree from the University of St. Thomas. After a long career, primarily in public health, she picked up writing poetry again. She lives in Lake Elmo.

DAVID RALPH JOHNSON resides in Lowertown Saint Paul with his wife, Theresa. Together they write, paint, and photograph the city from their tiny abode overlooking Mears Park.

PATSY KAHMANN lives in Minneapolis but has called many places home. Born in Kansas City, she and her family came to live on a farm near Granite Falls, Minnesota, in 1962. Her memoir, *House of Kahmanns*, is about forged and fractured family bonds. Her 2014 story was chosen for the ten-year retrospective. She is retired from the University of Minnesota, where she worked with student athletes and coaches in the women's basketball program.

LISA KASTE has been living in Saint Paul since 2010. She is a Native American mother, grandmother, and friend to many. Her hobbies include reading, watching documentaries, and going to music festivals. She works as a teaching assistant at the American Indian Magnet School in Saint Paul and as a homeless advocate during evenings and weekends at two shelters in Minneapolis.

SARAH KOPER writes poetry, fiction, and nonfiction. Her poem "Moonwalker" is engraved on a sculpture located at St. Cloud State University. "Baseball Bits #2" was published in *A View from the Loft* (2001). "Searching for Answers" was selected for Hazelden's Conference on Arts and Healing. Her first book is *Potholes: A Collection of Poems, Quotes & Cameos* (2008), which is available at the-liberal-prude .com. Her work has previously appeared in *Saint Paul Almanac*.

MICHEL STEVEN KRUG is a Minneapolis poet, fiction writer, and former print journalist from the Johns Hopkins Writing Seminars. He's the managing editor for *Poets Reading the News* literary magazine and litigates. His poems have appeared in *The Blue Mountain Review*, *Jerry Jazz Musician*, *MacQueen's Quinterly*, *Portside*, *The Brooklyn Review*, and more.

THOMAS LABLANC is a Dakota artist who lives in Saint Paul. He contributes to a world where we use creativity and options other than war, racism, classism, and exploitation to solve the problems that we all share by just being alive.

BETSY LEACH has been living and writing in Saint Paul since her last year of junior high school. She has worked in higher education and as a community organizer on Saint Paul's East Side for most of her adult life.

DIANA LEASKAS was born and raised and still lives in Saint Paul. She grew up in the Summit-University neighborhood beginning in 1977 and went to Central High School. She is married with two adult children and three cats. She has loved books and stories since she was two years old, and she began writing stories in the third grade. She LOVES creative writing and has a passion for it.

ARLETA LITTLE is a writer and culture worker. Her recent literary work has appeared in multiple publications, including *We Are Meant to Rise*, *Blues Vision: African American Writing from Minnesota*, *Saint Paul Almanac*, *Black Literacy Matters*, and *This Was 2020*. Her essay "Life and Death in the North Star State" was nominated for a Pushcart Prize. She is a co-author along with Josie Johnson and Carolyn Holbrook of *Hope in the Struggle: A Memoir* about the life of Josie Johnson. Arleta serves as the executive director for the Loft Literary Center.

VALERIE LITTLE studied creative writing and music at Pennsylvania State University. She has been published in *Kalliope*, *Aperture*, *Sheila-Na-Gig*, and a 2019 poetry anthology by Duck Lake Books. Professionally, she is a violist and orchestra librarian with the Minnesota Orchestra.

LILIA LOBOUGH is a senior at St. Catherine University, studying English and philosophy. One of her special talents is answering the question "So what are you going to do with that degree?" You can often find her running to catch a bus or buying too much sparkling water for her own good. Lilia lives with three wonderful roommates and, tragically, no dogs.

MARGARET PONDER LOVEJOY, EDD, a lifelong resident of the Rondo neighborhood, was taught by community elders to care for and love one another. This lesson has always lived in her heart: to care for the community. She has lived most of her life in the Rondo neighborhood and lives on the same property her parents bought before she was born.

RAYMOND LUCZAK is the author and editor of twenty-two books, including *Flannelwood* (Red Hen Press) and *Lovejets: Queer Male Poets on 200 Years of Walt Whitman* (Squares & Rebels). He lives in Minneapolis, Minnesota.

SARA MARTIN lives in Saint Paul with her husband, two sons, and their rescue mutt. When she's not spending time with her family or trying to sneak in writing time, she works as a public interest attorney. Her essays have appeared in *Adoptive Families* magazine and online in the *Peacock Journal, Mothers Always Write,* and the Star Tribune's *Cribsheet* blog.

LARRY D. McKENZIE ("SLIM") Bread and buttered in Chicago. Salt and peppered in the Twin Cities. He has been writing for more than forty years and currently working on *The Adventures of Saladeen.*

DAVID MENDEZ is a writer from Saint Paul's West Side working in education and in the community. He draws upon his blue-collar roots and Chicano experience in his works. He hopes to inspire others to take up the pen and share their stories.

JOHN MINCZESKI's poems have appeared in several previous editions of *Almanac*. He lives half a block from the border but spent almost thirty years living in the Lex-Ham neighborhood of Saint Paul.

NORA MURPHY is a fifth-generation Irish Minnesotan born in Imniza Ska almost sixty years ago. She is a mother, daughter, and appreciator of the river. Her latest book, *White Birch, Red Hawthorn*, explores her family's role in the genocide of Native nations in Minnesota and suggests pathways for healing.

AAROHI NARAIN is originally from New Delhi, India, and graduated from Macalester College in 2018. In her writing, she most enjoys covering food, arts, travel, and identity. She is currently based in Hong Kong, where she teaches English at an under-resourced youth college. Learn more at aarohinarain.com.

REBECCA NELSON works at East Side Elders, helping seniors stay in their homes as long as they are able to. She also serves on the boards of the Dayton's Bluff and Payne-Phalen community councils, the Payne Arcade Business Association, the American Indian Family Center, and the East Side Neighborhood Development Company, and is president of the East Side Lions Club. The East Side of Saint Paul is her passion.

LOREN NIEMI has spent forty years creating, collecting, performing, and teaching stories that matter. He is a published poet whose works include a chapbook, *Coyote Flies Coach*, and selections in the Poets Speak anthologies *Water*, *Walls*, and *Survival*. In 2019, Moonfire Publishing released his collection of ghost stories, *What Haunts Us*.

CATHERINE AYANO NIXON writes and sings songs about love, relationships, and life on earth, and also writes about healing the self through meditation and movement. She writes: "These days, my writing is often accompanied by one of my paintings."

YARA OMER is an educator. She works and lives in the Twin Cities. Yara writes in English and in Arabic.

MARJORIE OTTO worked for four years as a reporter and editor at Lillie Suburban Newspapers covering the East Side of Saint Paul. She says, "It was an honor to share the diverse stories of an original and tight-knit series of neighborhoods." Outside of writing, she loves being outdoors. She is a beekeeper, a paddler of rivers, and a hiker.

REGAN BYRNE PALMER lives in Minneapolis but grew up in Saint Paul. She co-founded and edited *Turtle Quarterly*, a literary magazine, and was a preliminary judge for the 31st Annual Minnesota Book Awards.

DEANNE L. PARKS is a painter, sculptor, writer, and speaker who builds the occasional giant puppet. Her work is published and collected internationally. She resides in Saint Paul's West End with her husband, their dog, and a ridiculous number of garter snakes.

HEIDI FETTIG PARTON is a wife, mother, and writer living in Stillwater, Minnesota. She received an MFA in creative nonfiction from Bay Path University. Her writing can be found in many publications, including *ENTROPY, Multiplicity Magazine, The Manifest-Station*, and the *Her Path Forward* anthology. Find her online at heidifettigparton.com.

JOSHUA PRESTON is a writer and historian whose work has appeared in *Minnesota History, Middle West Review, Popshot Quarterly*, and elsewhere. You can find him online at JPPreston.com.

JAMES SILAS ROGERS is a poet and essayist in Saint Paul. He's the author of a collection of poems, *The Collector of Shadows* (2019); a book about cemeteries, *Northern Orchards* (2014); and many notable essays.

KAREN SANDBERG lives in Minneapolis. Her mother grew up in Saint Paul on Goodrich Avenue, where she lived with her grandparents and every day watched her grandfather, the local doctor, drive off in his horse-drawn buggy to attend the sick and often the Little Sisters of the Poor, near their house. Karen has been published in *Main Street Rag*, *Vita Brevis*, and *Freshwater Literary Journal*.

HEIDI SCHALLBERG is an urban planner, writer, and walker. She wants you to calmly stop for people crossing the street when you are driving.

SEE MORE PERSPECTIVE (Adam Napoli-Rangel) has done years of youth work through hip-hop and spoken word dealing with social justice, identity, and community engagement issues; has performed at countless venues and festivals; and spoken at and facilitated workshops at various social justice conferences and retreats. SEE MORE aims to inspire and uplift through meditations on community, history, and the expression of pure imagination.

JULIA KLATT SINGER is the poet in residence at Grace Nursery School. She is the co-author of *Twelve Branches: Stories from Saint Paul* and author of four books of poetry. Her most recent, *Elemental*, has audio poems at OpenKIM (openkim.org). She's co-written songs with composers Craig Carnahan, Jocelyn Hagen, and Tim Takach.

GEORGE SLADE is a Saint Paul native and a Twin Citizen, and his daughters were both born in Saint Paul too. He is into photography. His father's Alzheimer's has taken his family down unforeseen and unforeseeable paths.

ANNETTE MARIE SMITH is an American author and poet and the founder/editor of *Facing Feminism*. Her two most recent books are *She Wanted Storms* and *Tell It to the Bees*. She is currently happily at work on a novel of magical realism set in Saint Paul.

As a refugee from Burma, MIN SOE SAN has gone through a profound life experience, which he interprets into poems. He led community classes by teaching Karen/Burmese, despite the noises of rifle fire. He barely escaped the militants after a house arrest in the village and somehow reached the Thai-Burma border. His family eventually arrived in Minnesota. During the long Minnesota winters, he would write down his poems in his notebooks, which he later transferred to a donated computer. Some he lost and some still remain.

Mexican Indigenous (Pirinda and P'urhépecha) and Chicana scholar and poet DR. GABRIELA SPEARS-RICO grew up in trailer parks and labor camps following the migrant farmworker trail along the American West Coast. She is a Stanford alumna and received a PhD from UC Berkeley. Her poetry has been published in various anthologies including *Sing: Poetry from the Indigenous Americas, Poesía mexicana en la frontera norte, Ethnic Studies Review, Feminist Anthropology,* and *Chiricú Journal: Latino Literatures, Arts, and Cultures.* In 2021, she was named a McKnight Land Grant Professor by the University of Minnesota.

DEBRA STONE writes short stories, poetry, and essays. She lives in Robbinsdale with her husband and their German boxer, Ziggy. Currently she is writing a novel.

ELIZABETH TANNEN is a writer, organizer, fundraiser, and educator based in Minneapolis. Her poems and essays have appeared in a range of publications, including *Copper Nickel, Front Porch Review, PANK, Southern Humanities Review, The Rumpus, Salon,* and elsewhere. Her manuscript *Notes on Distance* was one of five finalists for Milkweed's Lindquist & Vennum Prize for Poetry in 2018.

LEE COLIN THOMAS lives and writes in the Twin Cities. His poems have appeared in *Poet Lore, Salamander, Narrative, The Gay & Lesbian Review Worldwide, Pilgrimage, Water~Stone Review, Midwestern Gothic,* and elsewhere. Find him online at leecolinthomas.net.

MARY TURCK has published extensively as a journalist after working in a variety of jobs ranging from gym teacher to attorney. Her literary and journalistic blogs can be found at maryturck.com.

DR. ARTIKA R. TYNER is a passionate educator, poet, author, sought-after speaker, and advocate for justice. She is a prolific, award-winning author of adults' and children's books that include *Amazing Africa: A to Z* and *The Inclusive Leader: Taking Intentional Action for Justice and Equity.* In furtherance of her philanthropic efforts, she created Planting People Growing Justice Leadership Institute, a nonprofit organization committed to promoting literacy and diversity in books.

BETH L. VOIGT was born outside of Chicago, but Saint Paul has always been home. This is where her heart is and her family is, and as long as they are here, she will be here, writing about them. She has published essays in local and national publications, including *Saint Paul Almanac, Christian Science Monitor, Midwest Home, Minnesota Moments, Talking Stick,* and *Parenting.*

MIRIAM WEINSTEIN's chapbook, *Twenty Ways of Looking,* was published in 2017. Her poetry appears in the anthologies *The Heart of All That Is: Reflections on Home, Nuclear Impact: Broken Atoms in Our Hands,* and *The Little Book of Abundance,* and in several journals. She holds two master of education degrees from the University of Minnesota and a bachelor of arts degree from the University of Winnipeg.

CLARENCE WHITE is a writer, editor, typewriter poet, curator, and arts administrator. His publications are included in several editions of *Saint Paul Almanac, Suisun Valley Review, Public Art Review,* and *Martin Lake Journal,* and his essay "Smart Enough for Ford" appears in the anthology *Blues Vision: African American Writing from Minnesota.* He was the co-curator of the 2016 and 2017 Banfill-Locke Reading Series and Silverwood Park's 2014 Art on Foot. He is a past

Givens Foundation Retreat Fellow. Currently, Clarence is the associate director of the East Side Freedom Library and lives in Saint Paul.

MAE WHITNEY is a student moonlighting as a server. She has worked in restaurants for five years and has been carving away on projects and her education in her spare time.

DIANE WILSON, a Dakota writer, has published a memoir, *Spirit Car: Journey to a Dakota Past,* which won a 2006 Minnesota Book Award and appeared in the 2012 One Minneapolis, One Read program, and *Beloved Child: A Dakota Way of Life.* She was a 2013 Bush Fellow and 2018 AARP/Pollen Fifty Over Fifty honoree. Diane's latest novel, *The Seed Keeper*, won the 2022 Minnesota Book Award for Novel & Short Story.

TANAǦIDAŊ TO WIŊ | TARA PERRON is a Dakota and Ojibwe mother who grew up in Saint Paul, Minnesota. She studied Dakota language and culture at Metro State University. She is the author of *Takoza: Walks with the Blue Moon Girl, Animals of Khéya Wíta*, and *Animals of Nimaamaa-Aki.* Tara is inspired by the loving hearts of her sons; she is a creator and plant medicine enthusiast, and she believes in the healing power of storytelling.

DAWN WING is a librarian, multidisciplinary artist, and writer with interests in poetry, paper arts, painting, printmaking, sculpture, zines, comics, and collage. She enjoys creative experimentation with mixed media. Dawn is also a recipient of the 2022 Minnesota State Arts Board's Creative Support for Individuals grant to publish her next book, *Tien Fu Wu: Freedom Warrior.* Originally from New York City, Dawn has been a resident of Saint Paul since 2018.

ARON WOLDESLASSIE is a local stand-up, writer, and editor. You can find his work in *Mpls.St.Paul Magazine, The Nordly, Minnesota Playlist, Diaphora Media*, and many comedy clubs across the Twin Cities. When Aron isn't directly making art, he can be found reading, biking, or baking.

CHONG YANG was born to Hmong farmers and artists in Luang Prabang, Laos. Her family immigrated to Saint Paul in 1980, where she lived with her mom, Bai Vang, and siblings Yeng and Koua. Chong received her master's from the University of Minnesota College of Education and teaches high school English language arts in Saint Paul, where she lives. Chong has three wonderful daughters, Phaa-Der, Asha, and Kaia.

MEE YANG earned her master's in creative nonfiction from Hamline University. Her background is in language arts. She taught Hmong language at a charter school in Saint Paul for three years.

A native New Yorker (currently a Minneapolitan) **MARYAM MARNE ZAFAR** writes poetry that is reflective of local and world events. An artist who is a collage-lithographer, she has had her work acquired by the Metropolitan Museum of Art and become part of private collections. Her day job is as a graphic designer, brand strategist, photographer, and writer, partnering with museums and cultural organizations, nonprofits, small businesses, and other artists and writers to inform and cultivate positive relationships with their respective audiences.

JAMES ZIMMERMAN lives in the West Seventh neighborhood of Saint Paul with his three children. His writings have appeared in several issues of *Saint Paul Almanac*. He is the author of the book *Deliverance at Hand! The Redemption of a Devout Jehovah's Witness*.

KYRA ZIMMERMAN grew up in Minnesota and has been living in Saint Paul for four years. They are a University of Minnesota and Hamline alumni and currently a science teacher in Saint Paul. When not teaching, they enjoy aerial arts and adopting ferrets.

COMMUNITY EDITORS'
NOTES

Executive Editors

Wendy Brown-Baez

(2021-22) WENDY BROWN-BAEZ is the author of *Heart on the Page: A Portable Writing Workshop*. Her work has appeared in numerous literary journals and anthologies. She leads writing workshops in community spaces such as healing centers, libraries, prisons, and shelters. Wendy is a member of Minnesota Prison Writing Workshop, Writing to Wholeness Collective through the Minnesota Women's Press, and Eastern Shore Writers Association. This is her tenth year with Saint Paul Almanac because she believes in the power of words to transform lives.

Carolyn Holbrook

(2019) CAROLYN HOLBROOK is a writer, educator, and advocate for the healing power of the arts. Her memoir, *Tell Me Your Names and I Will Testify* won the 2021 Minnesota Book Award for Memoir & Creative Nonfiction. She is co-editor with David Mura of the anthology *We Are Meant to Rise: Voices for Justice from Minneapolis to the World.* She teaches at Hamline University and The Loft Literary Center and is a mother of five, grandmother of eight, and great-grandmother of two.

Project Administrator

Shaquan Foster

SHAQUAN FOSTER loves working with artists and community builders while creating works of his own, including serving as editor in chief of *Saint Paul Almanac*, managing and producing events like the Aardvark in the Park Festival, and serving on the board of Twin Cities Pride. In his free time, he is reading, writing, creating video game concepts, and co-hosting a film podcast.

Senior Editors

Marion Gómez

MARION GÓMEZ (she/her) is a poet and teaching artist based in Minneapolis. She has been awarded grants from the Minnesota State Arts Board and Intermedia Arts. Her work has appeared in *La Bloga*, *Mizna*, *Water~ Stone Review*, and *Saint Paul Almanac* among others. She is a program manager of awards and events at The Loft Literary Center.

Michael Kleber-Diggs

MICHAEL KLEBER-DIGGS is fascinated by mechanical things that are not powered by batteries. This is his second year serving as a senior editor for *Saint Paul Almanac*. Michael lives in Saint Paul with his wife, Karen, their two dogs, Jasper and Ziggy, and their two cats, Mocha and Curly. His book of poetry, *Worldly Things,* won the 2019 Max Ritvo Poetry Prize.

BEN WEAVER is a songwriter and poet who travels by bicycle. He uses his music as a tool to strengthen relationships between people and the land. Given the choice, he will side with the animals, lakes, rivers, and trees.

Ben Weaver

CLAUDETTE M. WEBSTER is a poet and essayist in the Twin Cities. A native of Jamaica, West Indies, she is curious and enjoys exploring her new home. An avid walker, she says you shouldn't be surprised if you find her walking in your neighborhood.

Claudette M. Webster

Ahmed Abdullahi   Leilani Andrews   Tomás Araya   Colleen Casey

Community Editors

AHMED ABDULLAHI is an alumnus of Higher Ground Academy. This was his second year with Saint Paul Almanac. When he isn't schooling people on the basketball court, he is reading a book, chilling with friends, or getting schooled on the court himself.

LEILANI ANDREWS loves to learn and experiment with life. When she's not working or in school, she enjoys the arts, such as writing, painting, photography, acting, and studying film. She doesn't know what she wants to do with her life yet but is excited for what the future may bring.

TOMÁS ARAYA is an architect and visual artist. This is his first time being a community editor for Saint Paul Almanac. He dedicates his time to the design and execution of public art projects, and his long-term career goal is to publish a series of graphic novels.

COLLEEN CASEY lives in a tiny sky-blue bungalow near Como Lake. She has turned her little yard into a paradise for birds, bees, butterflies, and other pollinators by planting it full of native wildflowers that bloom spring through fall. Of mixed Dakota and

Bridget Geraghty   Casey Gordon   Alia Jeraj   Melody Luepke

Euro-American heritages, she sees herself as a person of crosscurrents and confluences and believes we are all related.

BRIDGET GERAGHTY is an exhausted twenty-something who slings tea and sarcasm for a living. Despite a general disillusionment with the state of the world, she still manages to find magic in the written word. She hopes to start her own editing business and continue publishing her own writing.

CASEY GORDON has been in the Twin Cities for three years and is in her first year with Saint Paul Almanac. She has taught literature, writing, and changemaking at the City University of New York and the University of St. Thomas. She loves music and "Minnesota Experience" on TPT and has finally learned how to dress for the weather.

ALIA JERAJ is a vocalist, writer, and educator in the Twin Cities. She sings with groups including Nanilo, Artemis, and Mixed Precipitation. Her bylines include *POLLEN, Twin Cities Daily Planet,* and *American Craft.* By day she tutors math at a local high school.

MELODY LUEPKE no longer considers herself a newcomer to Minnesota, having weathered numerous seasons and adopted the

Khalid Mohamed   Kia Moua   Marjorie Otto

long Minnesota "o" in her speech. She is a grandmother, a newly-wed, and a consummate consumer of words.

This is **KHALID MOHAMED**'s second year as an editor for Saint Paul Almanac. Khalid is an alumnus of Higher Ground Academy. In his spare time, he likes to read books and play sports. His goal in the future is to become a pediatrician. When he first joined Saint Paul Almanac, he was shy, but he became more open.

This is **KIA MOUA**'s second year with Saint Paul Almanac. She is a published writer, community member, and humanist. Kia lives in Saint Paul with her family and their two furry babies, where she can be found reading nonfiction in her spare time. She hopes to be a published memoirist in her retirement.

MARJORIE OTTO is a writer and editor who spent four years as a journalist for a community newspaper on the East Side of Saint Paul. This is her first year as a community editor for Saint Paul Almanac. When she's not writing or editing, Marjorie can be found outdoors paddling on rivers, hiking, or beekeeping. Despite hating poetry as a kid, it's now her primary writing form, proving we can all grow and change.

Kathryn Pulley   Yusuf Sabtow   Ismail Sheikhomar   Frankie Weaver

KATHRYN PULLEY is mother of essays, fiery prose roaring from students' minds to soar across Google Docs. She prefers real dragon-based games and passes a mighty legacy of geekiness to her young daughter. Together, they may overcome the rational sensibility of her hitherto resistant husband and share their kingdom.

This is **YUSUF SABTOW**'s first year with Saint Paul Almanac. Yusuf is an alumnus of Higher Ground Academy with an internship at Be The Match®. He enjoys manga, anime, and a plethora of video games. Yusuf plans to pursue a degree that will land him a job in the technology field.

ISMAIL SHEIKHOMAR loves to put off school to chase his dream of becoming a software engineer. He has a mild addiction to caffeine but somehow is always tired. He enjoys tae kwon do and biking, but gaming is his true passion.

FRANKIE WEAVER is a seventeen-year-old from Saint Paul. In his free time, he likes to skateboard, draw, and play ultimate Frisbee.

Aron Woldeslassie   Alexa Yankton   Lisa Yankton

ARON WOLDESLASSIE is a local stand-up, writer, and editor. You can find his work in *Mpls.St.Paul Magazine, The Nordly, Minnesota Playlist, Diaphora Media*, and many comedy clubs across the Twin Cities. When Aron isn't directly making art, he can be found reading, biking, or baking.

ALEXA YANKTON is a member of the Spirit Lake Dakota. She delights in hiking nature trails, visiting museums, traveling, and being with her family. Alexa is a Pow Wow Princess and water carrier at ceremonies.

LISA YANKTON is a member of the Spirit Lake Dakota and a community organizer, educator, writer, and mother. At night she can be found stargazing. Instead of wishing on a star, she wishes she knew their names.

FUNDERS

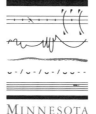

F. R. Bigelow Foundation
Marbrook Foundation
Mardag Foundation
McKnight Foundation
Metropolitan Regional Arts Council
Minnesota Humanities Center (MHC)*

Minnesota State Arts Board
Propel Nonprofits
Saint Paul Cultural Star Program
Saint Paul and Minnesota
    Foundation

*A note of gratitude to MHC for their partnership and generous gift that is reserved especially for the publication and related activities of *Saint Paul Almanac*, Volume 13: *A Path to Each Other*. We truly appreciate this opportunity to collaborate with MHC, given our aligned missions to foster understanding and collaborative action among individuals through the literary arts: "MHC uses philosophy, literature, civics, history, language & more to bring the humanities into the lives of every Minnesotan. Mission: connect our past, present, and future by bringing people together to increase understanding and spark change." mnhum.org/about-us/

COMMUNITY SUPPORTERS

*Neighborhood Businesses, Vendors,
and Nonprofit Support*

Afro Deli & Grill
Black Dog Cafe & Wine Bar
Davanni's
Foxy Falafel
Golden Thyme Coffee & Café
Jersey Mike's Subs
Naughty Greek
Rusty Taco
Dr. Sheronda Orridge Catering

Associated Bank
BankCherokee
Bicycle Theory Website Designer
CHS Field
In Black Ink
Next Chapter Booksellers
Public Art Saint Paul
Saint Paul Neighborhood Network
Smart Set
The University Club of Saint Paul
University of Saint Thomas
Walker|West Music Academy
WFNU Frogtown Radio

2020

Allen, Emilia Seay
Andrews, Becky
Avila, Kathleen
Bard, Paul
 In memory of Carol Connolly
Beltaos, Elizabeth
 In memory of Carol Connolly
Blechert, Tone
Bloom, Hella
Boland, Steve
Borchardt, Conie
Borer, Leo
Bren, Mary
Brombach, Ruth
Brown, Elizabeth G.
Brown-Baez, Wendy
Bryant, Katie
 In memory of Carol Connolly
Buchwald, Emilie
Burgeson, Jeremy
Bush, Christopher & Pamela
Callaway, Lindsey
Cannon, Tom & Charrelynne
Cassidy, Dawn
Castillo, Chris
Chau, Mey
Clairs, Lori
Coleman, Karlyn
Connolly-Rice, Katie
 In memory of Carol Connolly
Crosby, Christopher
Crowe, Bettie
Dalsin, Mary
Darling, Pat
Dempsey, Santana
Dingo, Sharon

DiSanto, Louis
Dittberner-Jax, Norita
Dovre Wudali, Sara and Mahadev
Downie, Jeremy
Elliott, Michael
Endalew, Sara
Fabia, Alyssa
Fajardo, Anika
Faricy, Carole
 In memory of Carol Connolly
Farr, Cecilia Konchar
Fee, Ellen
Fernandez-Williams, Sherrie
Fisher, Irene
 In memory of Carol Connolly
Fitzpatrick, Kevin
 Dearly Departed Friend
 Donated in memory of Carol Connolly
Flahavan, Judy
Fletcher Jr., Joe
Fletcher Sr., Joe & Betty
Fletcher, LaBridgette
Fontaine, Elizabeth
Foster, Yvonne
 In memory of Carol Connolly
Gagliardi, Annette
Garstka, Josh
Gibson, April
Gilats, Judy
Gomez, Marion
Gordon, Casey
Gordon, Kelly
Grotenhuis, Catherine & Steve
Guy, Tara
Hasse, Margaret
Hauer, Donna

Hazard, Mike
Hazard, Sonia
In tribute of Mother, Pat Olson, for
Mother's Day, Hebi & Hannah
Hendrikson, Jamie Lucke
Hirsch, Jordan
Holbrook, Carolyn
Hollen, David & Cynthia
In memory of Carol Connolly
Holt, Justin
Isaac, Donna
Johnson, Andrea E.
Johnson, Marlene
In memory of Carol Connolly
Jones, Geoff
Jones, Tish
Jurss, Jacob
Jurss, Leah
Kaba, Ibrahima
Kaplan, Steven
In memory of Carol Connolly
Kennedy, Joyce
Knight, Carla
Koefod, Susan
Komblum, Cinda
Krawczyk, Lisa
Lanphor, Molly
In memory of Carol Connolly
Latimer, Faith
Lauren, Jones
Lee, Sherry
Lee, Steven & Sia Vang
In memory of Gary Stoos
and Pam McAlister
Lees, Joanna
Lehman, Jonathan
Lindfors, Jonathan
In memory of Carol Connolly
Little, Arleta
Lorr, Don

Lotterman, Betty
Margolis, Eva
Mars, Amy
McGinnis, Shari
McKinnon, Ann
McRavin, Delano
In memory of Deb Torraine
Minczeski, John
Montalbono, Patricia
Moore, LaVonne
Moore, Sandy
Moreira, Judy
Murphy, Nora
Nabasi, Marta
Nakaoki, J.
Nelson, Larry
Nelson, Vickey
Nettell, Susan
Nightingale, Kelly
Nightingale, Kimberly
Odland, Jacob
O'Fallon, David
Oliker, Nancy
Olson, Pat
Orzechowski, Barbara
In memory of Carol Connolly
Otto, Marjorie
Palmer, Regan
Parton, Heidi
Pechauer, Mary
Peterson, Katherine
Peterson, Kathy
In memory of Carol Connolly
Pienta, Jill
Pieri, Paul
Pingel, Lucas
Pointer, Dr. Russell & Evangeline
Porter II, Louis
Ramstad, Marly
Runyon, Deb

Schiebout, Annette
Schuster, Margaret
Shahid, Sagirah
Sheehy, Colleen
Si-Asar, Rekhet
Simpson, Lori
Skemp, Vincent
Song, Rebecca
Speaker, Mary
Stone, Debra
Stone, Stewart
Stumpf, Heidi
Sturdevant, Lori
Swenson, Alice
Sylvester, Betsy
Thew, John
Tilsen, Barbara
Tilsen, Dan
Titus, Jake
Triplett, Janet
Tripp, Azania
Tripp, Hedy
Turner, Hubert & Mae
Tyner, Artika
Morningstar Ubbelohde, Nell
Ulrich, Suzan

Unowsky, David
Vagnino, Katie
Vang, Katherina
Vento, Susan
 In memory of Carol Connolly
Vongsay, Saymoukda
Waterman, Martha
Watts, Roger
Webster, Claudette
Weiss, David
Welch, Susan
 Dearly Departed Friend
Westbrook, Janie
Westbrook, Susan & William
 In memory of Carol Connolly
White, Clarence
Winfield-Hickman, Robin
Yarbrough, Valerie
Young, Patricia A.
Zafar, Maryam Marne

2020 Almanac Accolades
Sustaining Members

Brown, Elizabeth G.
Crowe, Bettie Foster

2021

Aiken, Ta-coumba
Bard, Paul
Borchardt, Conie
Brown, Elizabeth G.
Brown, Jewell
Burgeson, Jeremy
Bush, Christopher & Pamela
Cannon, Walter
Chatman, Mary

Chmielarz, Sharon
 In memory of Carol Connolly
Clabon, George
Coates, Almeda
Crowe, Bettie
DeCelle, Katharine
Dittberner-Jax, Norita
Doherty, Sharon
Dovre Wudali, Sara

Fletcher, LaBridgette
Fletcher Sr., Joe & Betty
Gaskill, Gayle
Gilats, Judy
Giles, Melvin
Grotenhuis, Catherine
Hasse, Margaret
Hazard, Mike
Hebron, Theresa
Henri, Gisele
Holt, Justin
Isaac, Donna & Matthew
Jones, Jenny
Jurss, Leah
Koefod, Susan
Ladson, Deborah
Lee, Steven & Sia Vang
Lenfestey, Jim
Little, Arleta
Lotterman, Betty
Lovejoy, Dr. Margaret
Maitland, Margaret Todd
McGinnis, Shari
McKinnon, Ann
Minczeski, John
Monaghan, Jennifer Holder
Monteith, Rick
Moore, Sandy
Nelson, Vickey
Nightingale, Kimberly
Parton, Heidi
Peters, Sarah
Pfeiffer, Paul
Pointer, Dr. Russell A. & Evangeline
Pulley, Kathryn
Rice, Brian F.
    In memory of Carol Connolly
Riveros, Sarah Degner
Runyon, Deb
Schultz, Kurt

Shahid, Sagirah
Sheehy, Colleen
Shelton, Lou Ann
Sims, John
Skemp, Vincent
Stone, Stewart
Sutphen, Joyce
Tilsen, Barbara and David
Tilsen, Dan
Trimble, Steve
Turck, Mary
Unowsky, David
    In memory of Carol Connolly
Vagnino, Katie
White, Clarence
Willow, Morgan Grayce
Yarbrough, Valerie
Zafar, Maryam Marne

2021 Almanac Accolades
Sustaining Members

Brown, Elizabeth G.
Bush, Christopher & Pamela
Crowe, Bettie Foster
DeCelle, Katharine
Farr, Cecilia Konchar
Hasse, Margaret
Holbrook, Carolyn
Holt, Justin
McGinnis, Shari
Moore, Sandy
Nightingale, Kimberly
Ratliff, Casey
Stone, Debra
Titus, Jake
Vagnino, Katie
Vongsay, Saymoukda
Webster, Claudette
Zafar, Maryam Marne

2022 WINTER AND SPRING

Clabon, George
Gilats, Judy
Gomez, Marion
Hamilton Triplett, Janet
Jandric, Thomas
Sheehy, Colleen

2022 Almanac Accolades
Sustaining Members

Ganesan, Mugunthan
Gause, Michael
Hale, Robert
Jensen, Lura
Johnson, Andrea E.
Waterman, Cary
Willow, Morgan Grayce

2021–2022 Almanac Accolades
Sustaining Members

Brown, Elizabeth G.
Bush, Christopher & Pamela
Crowe, Bettie Foster
DeCelle, Katharine
Farr, Cecilia Konchar
Hasse, Margaret
Holbrook, Carolyn
Holt, Justin
McGinnis, Shari
Moore, Sandy
Nightingale, Kimberly
Ratliff, Casey
Stone, Debra
Titus, Jake
Vagnino, Katie
Vongsay, Saymoukda
Webster, Claudette
Zafar, Maryam Marne

PLEASE VISIT OUR WEBSITE

saintpaulalmanac.org

COMMUNITY EDITOR APPRENTICESHIP
saintpaulalmanac.org/projects/community-editor-apprenticeship/

THE ALMANAC
saintpaulalmanac.org/projects/the-book/

STORYMOBILE
saintpaulalmanac.org/projects/storymobile/

RONDO DOCUMENTARY 1
Rondo: Beyond the Pavement
saintpaulalmanac.org/projects/rondo-beyond-the-pavement/

RONDO DOCUMENTARY 2
Rooted in Rondo
saintpaulalmanac.org/projects/rooted-in-rondo/

WRITING CONTESTS
saintpaulalmanac.org/projects/contests/

FOLLOW US ON SOCIAL MEDIA

Facebook: Saint Paul Almanac
Instagram: @saintpaulalmanac
Twitter: @stpaulalmanac
LinkedIn: The Saint Paul Almanac